D1798420

Contents

MANKIND
AT THE
CROSSROADS

John F. Sutcliffe, PhD, FInstP

To Charlie

Best wishes

John

ARTHUR H. STOCKWELL LTD.
Torrs Park   Ilfracombe   Devon
Established 1898
www.ahstockwell.co.uk

Arthur H. Stockwell Ltd., bear no responsibility
for the accuracy of events recorded in this book.

ISBN 0 7223 3551-2
Printed in Great Britain by
Arthur H. Stockwell Ltd.
Torrs Park   Ilfracombe
Devon

Foreword

At the beginning of the twenty-first century, it seems that humanity is heading for a major crisis. There have been crises in human affairs in times past, such as the Reformation, French Revolution, Industrial Revolution, but these have been limited to certain countries or regions. The crisis that faces mankind today is global and comes in the context of globalization, the information revolution and vast arsenals of weapons of mass destruction. Many would argue that the past two centuries have been marked by rapid and accelerating progress, in the acquisition of knowledge of the natural world and its application for the benefit of humanity. However, many of these proponents of science and technology ignore the spiritual dimension of man's existence and purpose, and it is the aim of this book to attempt to redress the balance in some degree. It is the imbalance that now exists between material progress and mankind's spiritual understanding, and the resultant imbalances in nature, that threaten mankind's continued existence upon this planet. When one considers that the timescale to effect the necessary changes could be as little as twenty years, the prospect of colonising another planet (such as Mars) is academic.

I am a reluctant author. There is a proliferation of books covering a whole variety of themes, such as New Age prophesies, legends of the past and their possible relevance to today's world crisis, the possibility that we have been at this crossroads in times past, and how there may be technical solutions to today's problems. So I ask myself why another book? Will this make the difference between the extinction of human life on this planet or the continuation of our civilisation in a changed form?

There are developments in scientific knowledge that offer the prospect of a new golden age, such as better health, greater longevity and greater abundance than previously known in recorded history. The application of the knowledge of the human genome to produce revolutionary treatments for genetically based diseases and disabilities. The development of artificial intelligence, using light as well as electricity offers even greater ability to communicate and conduct activities in hostile environments. Yet all these exciting developments have dangerous negative aspects which could threaten the existence of mankind.

Man is naturally inquisitive, and it is a natural tendency to tinker and meddle. The spectacular success of physical and biological sciences over the past three centuries is testimony to the scientific methodology of theories and models being based on experimental observation. Yet the observer today can see that all is not well with the state of the earth, and it is now realised that the phenomenon of global warming is predominantly due to human activities.

The most significant development is in the acceleration in the growth of the human population. This has placed a rapidly increasing burden on available finite resources, and the Western economic system, based on market growth, poses a serious threat to our continued existence. It is just being realised that our existence depends on the continued existence of other species, and as these are squeezed out to accommodate the demands of the human race, so we imperil ourselves.

The possibility of positive feedback mechanisms in the accumulation of atmospheric greenhouse gases implies that these changes could accelerate, and that humankind will have to adapt quickly to ensure continuity on this planet. This adaptation of our civilisation will be painful unless there is an appreciation of the spiritual dimension of life, which is generally unseen, has been ignored, and is fundamental to all life.

The text is divided into two parts. The first considers our present situation and its consequences. The second part analyses the mind-brain interface and considers the evidence for a fundamental spiritual aspect to life which underpins the physical world.

Part 1

Ecological imbalance: the population explosion

If a circle is drawn with a radius of 50m, the thickness of the inscribed line represents the biosphere, the limit of all known terrestrial life. This narrow spherical margin contains all known forms of life, distributed between the hydrosphere (the seas and oceans), the surface of the landmass and the atmosphere. Within the oceans are unknown multitudes of life forms and the range of species of life on land has still not been completely catalogued.

Man is at the top of an ecological pyramid which comprises four layers. At the bottom are the bacteria, fungi, algae, photoplankton and other microorganisms that fix nitrogen and other nutrients. This layer contains the largest biomass, even though most of it is invisible to the naked eye. These organisms support plant life in conjunction with the process of photosynthesis, whereby light is used by plants to synthesise carbohydrates from carbon dioxide and water and release oxygen to the atmosphere. Other microorganisms in the lowest layer of the ecological pyramid fix nitrogen from the air, to synthesise nitrates and proteins, and others concentrate phosphorus and sulphur, which promote growth in plants and which are used in bone structures, protein and the energy metabolism of animals and man. Plants in turn provide nutrition for herbivores which in turn support carnivores. Since man is omnivorous, he finds nutrition from (mostly) herbivores and plant life. The characteristic of the food chain is usually that the biomass in each layer of the ecological pyramid decreases at higher levels. The process of photosynthesis in plants ingeniously complements the metabolism of animals and man, in which carbohydrates are consumed by combustion with oxygen to produce energy, carbon dioxide and water. The life forms in the lower levels of the ecological pyramid recycle the waste from animals and man, completing an ecological cycle for which the only external power source is sunlight.

The sunlight which reaches the earth's surface is filtered by the atmosphere and ionosphere. The latter comprises high energy charged particles, emitted from the sun (the solar wind) and other parts of the cosmos, which would be hazardous to life if they were not trapped above the atmosphere by the earth's magnetic field. The action of this radiation causes oxygen (O_2) in the upper atmosphere to form the allotrope ozone (O_3), which filters out harmful ultraviolet radiation from the sun. Thus the light reaching the earth's surface has just sufficient energy to promote photosynthesis. The destruction of the ozone layer would admit ultraviolet radiation which would cause photodegradation of plant and animal life.

This ingenious self-sustaining mechanism for life on this planet is threatened by the accelerating growth of the human population. 2,000 years ago the human population was around 300 millions and the rate of growth was slow. 250 years ago the population had risen to only 800 millions, due to the high rate of infant mortality and miscarriages and a relatively short life expectancy. By 1800 the population reached one billion (thousand million) and doubled to two billion by 1930 due to improved infant survival and greater longevity. A third billion was added by 1960, a fourth by 1974, a fifth before 1990 and a sixth by 1998. Despite population decline in the former Soviet Union states due to disease and social decay, the world population is expected to pass eight billions by 2025.

The view of the earth from space, which came with the launching of space probes, the moon landings and the building of the space stations made it evident that the surface of the earth is finite. The burgeoning human population is straining the available resources to support life to breaking point. The clearing of tropical rainforests to provide more land for agriculture is an attempt to prevent mass starvation, and in so doing is destroying the habitat of many valuable species of animals and plants, the latter contributing significantly to the replenishment of the atmosphere with oxygen and removal of carbon dioxide. The agricultural land so gained rapidly loses its fertility due to erosion so that more rainforest needs to be felled to sustain food production. The lowest levels of the ecological pyramid are devastated by these developments since the microorganisms in the soil cannot sustain the demands made upon them. It is now recognised that the agricultural lands of the earth are losing their fertility, which implies that the biomass in the lowest level of the ecological pyramid is shrinking.

It is finally being realised that human activities are affecting the global environment significantly. The emission of carbon dioxide since 1950 has quadrupled due to increased power generation using fossil fuels, the abundance of cars, air travel, rocketry, forest clearances for agriculture and fires. The lifetime of carbon dioxide in the atmosphere is thought to be as much as one hundred years. Thus the effect of global warming due to retention of solar heat by increased levels of atmospheric carbon dioxide is likely to be delayed.

Changed climatic conditions will devastate wildlife which cannot adapt to the new conditions or relocate to areas that remain more agreeable to their normal habitat. It is likely that dry areas will become drier, wet areas will suffer more severe rainfall and flooding, and tropical diseases will invade temperate areas of the globe. Third World countries will be less able to compensate for these environmental changes and the death toll, of both animals and humans, will be heavy. This may be nature's way of controlling the burgeoning human population.

Western science is endeavouring to prolong life by researching the causes of ageing. What is being promoted as a desirable objective may in fact prove to exacerbate the problem of overpopulation.

Attempts at population control using contraception, voluntary sterilisation and clinical abortion of pregnancies have serious social consequences. Apart from contravening many social and religious customs, they threaten to dislocate these societies by reducing the number of young wage earners who then have to support an increasing burden of elderly citizens, who have greater life expectancy due to effective medical science. In developing countries, where there is no system of state welfare in retirement, the elderly have to rely directly on their offspring for support. This social arrangement has resulted in large families, which, in conjunction with reduced infant mortality, has caused an explosion in numbers. Attempts to impose limits on family size, such as in China's one child policy, have not been very successful, and in that country, the policy has not been so strictly enforced in rural areas. Presently China has approximately 1.3 billion people and

India's population has now passed the one billion mark and is growing more rapidly than in China.

The ominous situation suggests that either the human population is reduced voluntarily or else nature will ensure a holocaust of human numbers, through natural disasters, starvation and disease.

Physical changes: Antarctica Rising

The polar ice masses are the temperature regulator for the planet. An accumulation of heat is absorbed by melting ice from the poles and from glaciers, which keeps the global temperature approximately constant but would raise sea levels. Conversely, heat loss from the planet results in the freezing of polar water and causes sea levels to fall. The latent heat of fusion of ice is 80 calories per gram, enough to raise the temperature of one gram of liquid water from the freezing point to 80 degrees centigrade. Therefore the polar ice caps contain a huge thermal capacity, and the mean temperature of the oceans should not vary significantly.

The magnitude of waste heat emissions and carbon dioxide production due to human activities across the globe is now sufficient to disturb the global temperature equilibrium, particularly as carbon dioxide is a greenhouse gas, preventing the radiation of excess heat back into space. While there have been huge fires in past times that have destroyed forests and cities, these have been localised and have not been on a scale to affect the global equilibrium. The greenhouse gas emissions from electrical power generation, automobile exhausts, air travel, rocketry, forest clearances for agriculture and fires are of an unprecedented magnitude. It is believed the lifetime of carbon dioxide in the atmosphere could be as long as 100 years, and is removed predominantly by plants, in particular the tropical rainforests, and by dissolving in the oceans. Dissolved oxygen in the oceans provides respiration for fish and other sea life. However, if the temperature of the oceans were to rise significantly, both oxygen and carbon dioxide would be desorbed back into the atmosphere. This would put all ocean life at greater risk of asphyxiation and increase the abundance of

11

atmospheric greenhouse gas, increasing the retention of excess heat. Thus there is a major positive feedback mechanism inherent in the warming of the oceans, which would cause the greenhouse effect to accelerate except for the cooling effect of polar melt-water.

The analysis of the available evidence of warming of the oceans is complicated by the multitude of ocean currents, which may be disturbed from normal by polar and glacial melt-water. For example, Europe is made habitable and temperate by the Gulf Stream, originating in warm Caribbean waters, but if this were diverted southwards by Arctic melt-water, the European climate could suddenly become more severe. Thus the effect of global warming may actually cause certain regions to become colder, or more extreme in temperature variations between summer and winter. Also this would affect seasonal rainfall, becoming heavier in the wetter seasons but drier at other times. Thus heavier precipitation than normal would lead to flooding. This seems to be the pattern we are observing.

Satellite measurements of mean ocean temperature suggest a rise of 0.6 degrees centigrade at the present time. This may seem small, but due to polar melt-water, a large increase is not expected, but this small increase in itself will exacerbate the greenhouse effect by desorbing dissolved gases from the oceans. If this is confirmed, it will be detrimental to sea life, and fish stocks will diminish due to asphyxiation. Since sea life is a major source of food for an expanding human population, starvation will be the result. Thus for a given level of reabsorption of carbon dioxide by plant life by photosynthesis, only the cooling effect of polar and glacial melt-water will prevent an acceleration in the further rise of ocean temperature and hence global temperature.

Apart from carbon dioxide and other "greenhouse gasses" such as methane, another culprit for global warming, could be water vapour itself. If ocean temperatures are increasing, there will be more evaporation, increasing atmospheric moisture, and more precipitation will result. Human activities are now producing more waste heat than ever before. Every power station, car and aircraft wastes around half of the fossil fuel energy as heat. It is well known that dull overcast nights are generally warmer than nights with clear skies. Thus atmospheric water vapour will tend to trap heat generated from human activities, and city and urban areas are generally warmer than rural areas due to the concentration of heat sources. The magnitude of heat generation from all sources of fuel consumption worldwide is now sufficient to raise the mean temperature, particularly if the waste heat is not being radiated out into space as efficiently due to changed atmospheric conditions.

Paradoxically, "dirty" pollution of the atmosphere may cause global cooling. This is evident after large volcanic eruptions such as the recent eruption of Mount St Helens in Washington State on 18th May 1980. It has been observed that "dirty" atmospheric pollution, containing carbon particles and sulphates, reflect incoming solar radiation back into space very efficiently and inhibit the formation of clouds, thereby allowing waste heat from the ground to be radiated into space. Likewise, airborne sand particles prevent cloud formation and inhibit rainfall so that deserts tend to remain deserts. However, where there is a localised heat source, such as a power station, the rising hot "dirty" polluted air causes an inrush of cold adjacent air that can result in sudden and heavy precipitation. Conversely, "clean" atmospheric pollution would be more effective in promoting the greenhouse effect since it is less likely to inhibit the formation of clouds of sufficiently large water droplets which can fall as rain.

At the present time there are approximately 20,000 commercial flights per day. The carbon dioxide and water vapour trails from high flying aircraft, at altitudes of over 10,000 metres, are likely to be very effective in trapping heat in the atmosphere, and would persist for considerable periods since they are beyond the reach of plant life, algae and phytoplankton to absorb them. Only atmospheric convection currents and precipitation from high altitudes would bring these gases to ground and sea level where they could be removed. It could take hundreds of years to remove these high altitude greenhouse gases effectively.

Thus it seems that traditional "dirty" pollution from wood and coal burning might actually cool the planet, but more recent "clean" pollution and high altitude greenhouse gases are more effective in trapping heat.

The earth is flattened at its poles and distended at the Equator due to the centrifugal forces on the crust produced by its rotation. The South Pole is flattened more than the North Pole due to the mass of ice resting upon the Antarctic continent (the Arctic polar ice sheet is floating). As the polar ice sheet melts to regulate the mean temperature of the oceans, the reduced mass of ice will permit the Antarctic tectonic plate to float upwards on the semiliquid mantle relative to the adjoining plates. This will have two gradual but significant consequences:

1) Water will be displaced northwards. Sea levels will rise more than expected, particularly in the northern hemisphere. This would be partly offset by a similar rise of icebound arctic landmasses, which nevertheless comprise a much smaller area than Antarctica. Low lying coastal areas will be flooded, including major population centres, and millions of people will be displaced.

2) The equilibrium of the forces at the boundaries between tectonic plates will be disturbed, resulting in an increased incidence and magnitude of earthquakes and tsunamis (where these occur underwater). The latter in conjunction with rising sea levels will severely disrupt major population centres since the tsunamis will be sudden and unexpected.

Coastal ice shelves that break away from Antarctica will not raise sea levels significantly because they displace their own weight of water already. However, where land is exposed at the fringes of the continent and at mountain tops, the rate of melting will accelerate due to the reduced albedo (reflectivity of sunlight) relative to ice. Since it is the ice layer underneath in contact with the land mass that will melt first (due to pressure), frictional forces holding the ice in place will be reduced, causing it to shift and collapse. A collapse into the sea will cause tidal waves with possible consequences like a tsunami. The shifting and collapsing of ice will expose more land and cause the heating process in Antarctica to accelerate.

Presently there is an unstable dormant volcano on La Palma in the Canary Isles, whose western flank threatens to split apart and slip into the Atlantic Ocean at the next eruption or earth movement. This slip of around 500 billion tons of rock into the ocean would generate a huge tsunami, a 50m high tidal wave that would hit the eastern coast of the United States a matter of four hours later. Everything up to 20km inland would be destroyed by this wave, including all the coastal cities. The question to be asked is not if it will happen but when. A similar event occurred around 100,000 years ago off the coast of the island of Hawaii, creating a tsunami along the Queensland coast of Australia, 7,000km away. The tidal wave was estimated to have been 100m high, washing coastal debris many kilometres inland. Luckily there was no human habitation there at that time.

The ice masses on Antarctica and Greenland contain a climatic history of the planet going back millions of years. The deeper ice is more ancient. The analysis of ice cores bored through the ice, both on Greenland and in Antarctica, have shown that climate changes in the past have been dramatic and sudden, if infrequent. The last was dated approximately at 65 million years ago, when it is believed that the collision of an asteroid with the surface of the earth caused the dinosaurs to become extinct. The suddenness of this climate change in history suggests that if the planetary balance is disturbed, wild oscillations in the climate can occur before a new equilibrium is restored. More recently, the woolly mammoths of Siberia and North Canada were extinguished by a sudden and very rapid cooling of the northern climate. The mass of these well preserved carcases in the arctic tundra suggests that a severe chill, with temperatures well below normal, was the cause of the extinction. The thermal capacity of a mammoth carcase would require extreme cooling for the innermost parts not to putrify before freezing. Thus here is evidence that wild oscillations in climatic conditions can occur when the global climatic balance is disturbed.

How we got here: the magicians

The understanding, conquest and exploitation of the material world that has been achieved by the beginning of the twenty-first century shows the spectacular success of the methods of science and technology, which began around 500 years ago. To people of that time, the scientists and technologists of today would appear to be veritable magicians.

For 1,500 years the Western world was dominated by the patriarchal Christian Church, centred on the Pope in Rome. Of around fifty gospels written concerning the events at the heart of Christianity, only four were included in the New Testament of the Bible. The Council of Nicea in AD330, under the chairmanship of the emperor Constantine, made certain cuts to these gospels to eliminate any undesirable ideas and influences. Any heretical thinking was severely punished, as a deterrent to others. Despite this, an underground alternative to the Church existed, in the form of the Knights Templar, the Cathars of southern France, the Priory of Sion and various forms of Freemasonry and Rosicrucianism. These movements questioned the validity of Church doctrine and venerated such figures as John the Baptist and Mary Magdalen, whom they claimed had been denied their true significance.

The authority of Christianity was seriously challenged in the sixth century by the rise of Islam, which was excluded from Europe except for the Moorish occupation of Spain and southern France. The rivalry between these two great Western religions was manifest in the conflict over Jerusalem and the Holy Land in the eleventh, twelth and thirteenth century crusades and has continued since.

The Knights Templar and the Cathars were ruthlessly exterminated in the fourteenth and fifteenth centuries after the

16

Moors had been expelled from Europe. However, the power of the Church was broken by the invention of printing in 1455 by Johann Gutenberg (1400-68) and the Protestant Reformation in the early sixteenth century. The literate man and woman was able to discern that the practices of the Church were corrupt, at variance with biblical teaching, and so began a long process of independent thought. Even in those parts of Europe where the Catholic Church remained in control, there was a gradual awakening of new ideas.

The traditional and most ancient science was astronomy, dating back to ancient Babylon, Egypt and Greece. (It is now realised that the positions of the ancient pyramids in relation to the River Nile reflected the positions of the stars of Sirius in relation to the Milky Way at that time.) The Church doctrine of the geocentric universe was challenged by the observations of the new astronomers, Galileo (1564-1642), Nicolaus Copernicus (1473-1543), Tycho Brahe (1546 -1601) and Johannes Kepler (1571-1630). From these scientists came the familiar model of the solar system, with laws governing planetary motion. Despite early attempts by the Church to suppress these new ideas, the philosophy of basing models of the universe on observation took hold across Europe. Astronomy made little further progress until the application of spectroscopy in the nineteenth century, from which the composition of the stars was found to be the same as our sun. The observation of Doppler shifts in the spectral emissions from stars revealed that the apparently stationary stellar background was moving away from us, with the most distant stars moving most rapidly. Scientists concluded from this observation that the universe must have started with a colossal explosion, now called the Big Bang.

The experiments of Galileo and Sir Isaac Newton (1642-1727) produced the laws of mechanics, and the latter played a very significant part in the development of optics and the mathematics of calculus. Newton was also an alchemist and spent many years investigating the possibility of a hidden code in the text of the Old Testament of the Bible. The latter was unravelled recently with the aid of computers, deciphering the original unpunctuated Hebrew script. (More will be said about this later.)

Within Europe, a system of skilled artisans had arisen, with membership of various guilds to perpetuate the skills. In central Europe this involved manufacture of clocks and watches, glass making and optics, textiles and dyes, stonemasonry, metalwork

B

and carpentry. Thus there was an industrial infrastructure that was receptive to the new technologies as they were introduced. Machinery that was water powered in the eighteenth century became steam powered in the nineteenth century and powered by electricity in the twentieth century.

Alchemy became chemistry as elements were isolated, identified and characterised. John Dalton (1766-1844) was the originator of the idea of chemical elements distinguishable by different weights. Antoine Lavoisier (1743-94) and Joseph Priestley (1733-1804) are both credited with the discovery of oxygen and explained the nature of combustion. It was Dmitri Mendeleyev (1834-1907) who organised the elements into a periodic table according to their properties from which those of unknown elements could be predicted. These developments allowed the creation of new and better materials; fibres, explosives, drugs and dyestuffs were required in an increasingly industrialised society. In this development German chemists were prominent, such as Justus von Liebig (1803-73), who pioneered quantitative organic chemical analysis. Large coal reserves provided the raw materials for experimentation, spawning large industries. There was no consideration of the environmental impact of these activities, and lung infections from inhaling polluted air were very common.

The work of Michael Faraday (1791-1867), William Kelvin (1824-1907) and James Clerk Maxwell (1831-79) were most significant in the development of electrical technology. They showed the relationship between electricity and magnetism and derived the laws governing it. As with the application of steam power to transport and industry, there were technologists and entrepreneurs ready to apply the new science of electromagnetism which revolutionised society. Heinrich Hertz (1857-94), Guglielmo Marconi (1874-1937), Thomas Alva Edison (1847-1931), Alexander Graham Bell (1847-1922), John Logie Baird (1888-1946) and Nikola Tesla (1857-1943) were just some of the prominent figures in this revolution which laid the foundation of today's mass communication and the internet.

Charles Babbage (1792-1871) was a century ahead of his time. His construction of a mechanical computer spawned a high precision engineering industry and anticipated the invention of the electronic computer in 1942 by J. G. Brainerd, J. P. Eckert and J. W. Mauchly and the transistor by William Shockley in 1948. Today's microelectronic revolution and the personal computer resulted from this discovery in solid state physics and the necessary miniaturisation required to reduce the weight of payloads in rocketry. This illustrates how a good idea rapidly gets application, and has revolutionised all walks of life.

Flight has had a long history. From the ancient Greek legend of Icarus to Leonardo da Vinci, designs of aircraft have been modelled on birds, but it was the invention of the internal combustion engine by Karl Benz (1844-1929) in 1885 and diesel engine by Rudolf Diesel (1858-1913) ten years later that produced a source of power that was also sufficiently light to make flight possible in a heavier than air machine. The First World War accelerated the development of aircraft as warfare extended into the third dimension. At about this time Robert Goddard (1882-1945) designed the first practical rocket and this was developed by Wernher von Braun (1912-77) and Herman Oberth in Germany during the Second World War to add a new and terrifying dimension to the conflict. The invention of the jet engine by Frank Whittle (1907-96) in 1937 revolutionised air transport.

The dawn of the twentieth century appeared to suggest that the laws of physics had explained the entire working of the universe. The only anomalies were the photoelectric effect, black body radiation and the constant velocity of light in free space regardless of the velocity and direction of the observer. Radioactivity was discovered by Henri Becquerel (1852-1908) in 1895 and radium was isolated from uranium ore by the Curies (Pierre, 1859-1906, and Marie, 1867-1934). The discovery of X-rays by Wilhelm Röntgen (1845-1923) in 1895, the quantum theory by Max Planck (1858-1947) and the general and special theories of relativity by Albert Einstein (1879-1955) completely revolutionised physics. Niels Bohr (1885-1962) and Ernest Rutherford (1871-1937) created a model of the atom akin to a miniature solar system with electrons orbiting the nucleus in quantised energy levels. However, Werner Heisenberg (1901-76), Erwin Schrödinger (1887-1961) and Wolfgang Pauli (1900-58) showed that fundamental particles behave not just like matter (having mass and momentum), but also like energy (having wavelengths and uncertainty of position and momentum or of time and energy). The very act of observing them disturbed the observation. Thus the precision of experimental observation became limited at the atomic level. From studies of the atomic nucleus Enrico Fermi (1901-54), Leo Szilard (1898-1964), Paul Dirac (1902-84), Albert Einstein, J. Robert Oppenheimer (1904-67) and others realised that it was possible to release the potent energy stored there if heavy nuclei could be made to fission. This proved to be easier than expected and the Second World War proved to be the stimulus for development of the first nuclear reactor and the atomic bomb. This technology has caused more controversy than any other due to its biological and environmental hazards. However it is in the genetic technologies that the greatest controversy lies.

The two main developments in the life sciences up to the twentieth century were made by Charles Darwin (1809-82), in 1858 postulating the evolution of species in response to their environment and Gregor Mendel (1822-84) in his study of genetics. Darwin's theory remains controversial today since it conflicts with fundamentalist religious beliefs in a divine creation of man. The great revolution in life sciences came with Watson, Crick, Franklin and Wilkins' discovery in 1951 that genetic characteristics were carried in the cell nucleus, in the structure of the DNA double helix molecule. The application of robotic analysis of the human DNA has now unravelled the base sequence of this molecule. The task facing life scientists now is to understand the significance of each part of the sequence and their impact on genetic characteristics. From this it is expected that hereditary diseases will be cured and the genetic ageing factor may be retarded or even eliminated. This line of development also raises alarming possibilities of human cloning, of which more will be said later.

Medical science made advances with the discovery of antiseptics by Joseph Lister (1827-1912) in 1867, and of anaesthetics (ether in 1842, local anaesthesia in 1885 and spinal anaesthesia in 1898) where hitherto surgical procedures risked sepsis and great pain. One of the most significant developments was the introduction of inoculation against smallpox by Edward Jenner in 1796, followed by vaccination against rabies in 1885 by Louis Pasteur and poliomyelitis in 1953 by Edward Salk. Thus the science of immunology was developed. Worldwide inoculation against malaria, tuberculosis, influenza and poliomyelitis have reduced the incidence of these diseases dramatically to a point where smallpox and poliomyelitis were considered to be completely eradicated. However, the excessive use of antibiotics and poor social conditions (particularly in parts of the former Soviet Union) have allowed new and more virulent strains of tuberculosis and malaria to appear. The quest for a vaccine against the HIV virus that causes AIDS (acquired immune deficiency syndrome) is ongoing, while the virus is rampant in many central and southern African countries and in south-east Asia, killing large proportions of the populations and causing severe social disruption.

The common factor in the qualities of these eminent scientists is careful observation, experimentation and logical derivation of laws based on these experiments. Many of the early scientists had considerable practical skills in building their own equipment. Experiments had to be reproducible under the same conditions, and any anomalies that were not due to experimental errors necessitated a revision of the theory. This method has served scientists well in unravelling the laws of the physical universe. The application of technology based on these laws has impacted on every aspect of Western life, revolutionising transport, communications, health care and the methods of warfare and defence. The latter have stimulated rapid technological development.

Each discovery found rapid application and the resulting technology formed the basis of new industries, yielding handsome profits for perceptive entrepreneurs. For example, the use of X-rays for treatment of cancers was carried out within months of their discovery in 1896 and diagnostic radiology started shortly after. The telegraph, the telephone and satellite telecommunication followed rapidly from their discovery.

The rapid increase in scientific knowledge which spawned new technologies created a need for more abundant raw materials and markets for the manufactured products. Exploration of new continents in the sixteenth and seventeenth centuries led to colonisation of these territories and exploitation of their populations and resources. This process was assisted by the emigration of the surplus European population to these territories. Thus at the beginning of the twentieth century, one quarter of the landmass was ruled by the British (excluding the United States of America), another quarter by Russia and slightly smaller areas were controlled by French, Spanish, Portuguese and Dutch colonialists. These covered the entire Western hemisphere and Oceania and nearly all of Africa and south and east Asia. Most of these territories gained political independence during the twentieth century (since the colonial powers did not have resources for this kind of control) but economic dominance remains with the former colonial powers and the USA. The national debt of many of the former colonies (owed to the former colonial powers) now consumes most of their wealth production, so that these countries are caught in self-perpetuating poverty, and they continue to provide cheap raw materials that allow the former colonisers to remain wealthy. Since the West controls the market, they dictate the terms of its operation. Globalisation has come to mean multinational companies, in league with Western governments, exercising control of the international economy, especially since the collapse of the Soviet Union. The two exceptions to this pattern of exploitation are the oil rich states of the Persian Gulf and the fringe countries of south-east Asia (Japan, Korea, Singapore, Taiwan, Thailand, Hong Kong, the Philippines, Indonesia and Malaysia), where the West encouraged new industrial developments as an economic bulwark against the spread of Communism from the Soviet Union and China. These nations have developed into a powerful economic bloc rivalling the United States and Europe. However, at the time of writing these economies seem to be in trouble and political instability and ethnic and religious violence are increasing.

There are parallels between the present situation and the situation at the beginning of the twentieth century. A revolution in physics and engineering was imminent then, Britannia ruled a quarter of the world and there was great optimism. This was the beginning of mechanised road transport, flight, telecommunications and atomic and nuclear physics. The Great War of 1914-18 revealed technology that had been developed in the American Civil War (1861-65) but was fought using outmoded strategies and the consequent devastating loss of life cast a huge shadow over Western civilisation. The influenza epidemic that followed killed even more people than the war. Today physicists are trying to devise a grand unified theory of the universe, to reconcile the strong electronic and nuclear forces with the weak force of gravity, the quantum theory of the subatomic world with the relativistic immensity of cosmos. We are aware that a repeat of the same events in this century as in the last would probably eliminate humanity from the planet, such is the potency of the weaponry now in existence. Since there is no mechanism whereby mankind may forget how to construct such weapons, peace making has become a continual necessity for the survival of our civilisation on earth. The fact that humanity moves from one crisis to the next shows that there is a deficiency in perception and understanding, even though we are more knowledgeable than ever before. Therefore it may be asked if the rapid scientific and technological development of the last two centuries has really been progress?

There are many who would attribute the lack of spiritual progress and understanding to the fall-off in religious adherence in the affluent Western world in the face of materialistic achievement. Yet in those medieval times when the Church held all authority and wealth, life was hard, brutal and short. Religions have been the cause of warfare and still threaten to trigger conflict, since they divide people from each other. The magicians of the scientific and technological world have no answer to this problem other than technological tricks to provide better security. For every trick and device, the opposing side will endeavour to circumvent it. And so the battle of wits continues. This is well illustrated by the efforts made to assure the security of the financial system and the internet at the present time. In a world of globalisation, chaos ever threatens to get the upper hand. The antics of mankind illustrate abundantly that the scientific and technological progress of the last two centuries has not been tempered and balanced by a corresponding spiritual growth. Therein lies the greatest danger.

Part 2

The mind-brain interface

It is usually considered that the human brain is at the pinnacle of the natural evolutionary process. 1.5 kilograms of soft tissue, comprising 100 billion (10^{11}) neurons or nerve cells, encased in the protective skull, and linked to five types of sensory input that give us awareness of the physical world, are considered to be the residence of our personality and character. The body provides the life-support system for the brain, physical locomotion and the means to manipulate objects in our environment. In essence modern science considers the mind and brain to be synonymous.

Nuclear technology has found many applications in late twentieth century medicine. The annihilation of antimatter positrons is used to produce dynamic physiological images of the brain in which certain mental activities can be associated with certain regions. Thus the subject of this experiment can be asked to listen to music or solve a mathematical problem and those associated parts of the brain show increased activity as glucose labelled with a positron emitting isotope is drawn to these areas and consumed. The positron annihilation radiation, in the form of two gamma rays travelling in opposite directions are detected on opposite sides of the subject's head and used to create an image of activity in the brain. Any abnormalities of brain function, due to a stroke or haemorrhage, can be located by the absence of normal activity. This nuclear technique, used in conjunction with computed tomographic imaging of the brain, is a powerful tool for doctors and neurologists, since anatomical and physiological images can be superimposed.

Sight

The sensory system attached to the brain is most remarkable. The retina of the eye comprises over 100 million photo-receptors, 110 million rods and 6 million cones, the former operative at low levels of illumination and the latter being concerned with colour vision in daylight. The cones comprise three kinds of cells, sensitive to red, green and blue light. The perception of other shades of colour is produced by the brain's analysis of the relative signals from the three types of cones.

The optic nerve comprises over one million nerve fibres packed into a cylinder only about 2mm diameter, a packing density far surpassing that of optical fibres used in present day telecommunications. These optic nerves transmit signals to the brain from over 100 times as many photo-receptors, which are linked together in a complex fashion. The rods are very sensitive, and several are linked to each optic nerve to reduce "noise" at low illumination. A noise free optical signal results from the reception of several light photons over a period of about 20 milliseconds, and there is a time lag of up to 0.3 seconds between reception of the photons and emission of the electrical signal, allowing a complex process of amplification to occur. By contrast, the less sensitive cones respond more rapidly, with a time lag of around 75 milliseconds between reception of a light photon and the production of an electrical signal.

The iris of the eye limits the amount of light entering the eye, so that a dynamic range of illumination of 10^{12} (one million million) times can be accommodated. The signals from the left half of each eye go to the left hemisphere of the brain and the signals from the right half of each eye go to the right hemisphere of the brain. Thus each hemisphere receives two half images, each half image being slightly different views, which the brain correctly combines to give a full field of view with depth. Distance vision derives from the differences between the views of each eye.

Hearing

Each ear comprises three parts, the outer, middle and inner ear. The outer lobe acts as a collector of sound, and reflections from different parts of the lobe produce minute delays (less than one millisecond) in reception at each eardrum which the brain can interpret to locate the distance and direction of the source. The drum is linked to the inner ear by three minute bones which effectively transmit any vibration to the fluid filling of the inner ear. This mechanism of the middle ear transmits sound very efficiently (air vibrations tend to be reflected at the surface of a liquid) from the air to the liquid filled inner ear, and amplifies it around sixty times.

The chambers of the inner ear are lined with 15,000 hairs attached to auditory nerves cells, arranged in four parallel rows, 32mm long having a width of 1/20th mm, and are tuned to respond to different frequencies, from 30Hz at one end to between 10kHz and 20kHz at the other. The amplitude of vibration of the hairs is as little as 10 pico-metres, (just a few atomic diameters). Thus the brain determines the pitch of any sound by the position at which receptor cells are most excited. The dynamic range of sound that can be heard varies from a threshold of 10^{-16} to 10^{-4} watts/cm2, a factor of one million million times. The lower limit is made possible by the ear generating its own low level sound and detecting interference from faint external sources, which has the effect of increasing the level of amplification.

Smell
There are between 10 and 25 million olfactory receptor cells, covering an area of 5cm2 inside the nose. Molecules which cause odours are captured by these receptor cells in the mucous membranes, in which different odour causing molecules are captured by specific receptors. The condition for capture by a specific receptor cell depends on the shape of the odour molecule. The threshold for detection of certain substances can be as low as one tenth of a pico-gram, and in dogs this threshold is much less (dogs have up to 220 million olfactory receptor cells, ten times the number in humans).

Taste
The surface of the tongue contains most of the taste receptor cells, which respond to sweet, sour, salt and bitter components of any substance. All flavours are made up of varying proportions of these four components. The taste buds or papillae, of which there are between 5,000 and 10,000 on our tongues, are highly sensitive to bitter substances, which may be toxic and therefore hazardous. Each papilla is about 70 microns high and 40 microns across and has

several taste buds on its surface. In addition there are chemical receptors in mucous membranes of the eyes, mouth, nose and throat which react to irritants, which result in the secretion of tears, mucous and saliva as a protective response.

Touch

The entire skin surface of the body is sensitive to touch, with an area of around 1.6 square metres. On average one square centimetre of skin contains 5,000 sensory corpuscles, 200 pain receptors, 25 pressure points, 12 cold sensitive and 2 heat sensitive points, 6 million cells, 100 sweat glands and 15 sebaceous glands. The greatest density of sensory cells is found on the surface of the hands and face and lower density on the back, with greater or lesser sensitivity to touch, temperature and pain.

The dermis with a thickness of one to two millimetres contains the hair follicles, nerve ends, sweat glands as well as blood capillaries and lymph glands. It is thickest on the palms of the hands and soles of the feet and thinnest in the armpits and eyelids. It provides a barrier against infection, mechanical damage, regulation of body temperature, secretes oil which lubricates the epidermis and hair and around 2% of respiration (oxygen-carbon dioxide gas exchange) occurs through the skin.

The response to stimuli is curious. Light stimulation of a sensitive area such as stroking around the eye with feather will produce a strong reaction in the subject. However, a severe blow may cause numbness as if the local sensory system shuts down. This is illustrated by soldiers who have been shot and not realised they had been hit until they see blood. The brain responds to severe stimuli by generating natural pain killers or endorphins.

The brain and nervous system

The nervous system comprises complex networks of nerve cells that link all parts of body to the brain. The larger nerve cells can be up to 0.2mm diameter and have extensions (processes) over 1m in length, but only a few micrometres across. These processes link to other nerve cells through junctions known as synapses, in which signals are transferred through neuro-transmitting substances such as dopamine, serotonin and acetylcholine. The hundred billion cells of the brain may each have several thousand synaptic connections to other neurons. In the development of the brain in the human foetus, neurons are formed at the rate of one quarter of a million per minute. At birth, although almost all neurons have been formed (to serve a lifetime) most interconnections have not yet been created. This occurs mostly in the first two years of life, where external stimuli through the senses plays a major role in their formation. (Contrast this with the creation of an electronic brain where all memory elements are initially connected but some connections are selectively destroyed by a laser to create the programme that will determine its operation.) With between ten thousand and fifty thousand connections per nerve cell, the total length of nerve fibres interconnecting the brain is over half a million kilometres. The nerve fibres that link the brain to all parts of the body carry signals at speeds of 40m/sec.

The human body contains around 150 grams of potassium and 100 grams of sodium. These are vital trace elements for the operation of the nervous system. Potassium exists almost entirely within cells and sodium outside cell membranes. The transmission of signals along nerve fibres is accomplished by exchanging sodium and potassium across the neural membrane. After transmission the nerve recovers by pumping potassium back inside and sodium to the outside, so that it is cocked, ready to fire again. Each impulse travels at the same speed and the intensity of the stimulus depends on the frequency with which impulses are transmitted. These impulses can be followed with suitable apparatus and electrodes attached to the skin where a change in electrical potential can be oberved. Millions of such signals passing along nerve fibres generate an electromagnetic field.

At each synapse, signals are transferred from one neuron to others by neuro-transmitter substances such as dopamine, serotonin and acetylcholine. These neuro-transmitters, of which there are more than thirty, have specific molecular shapes that engage with molecules on the opposite surfaces of each synapse, akin to a lock and key arrangement and trigger a signal in the neuron. A deficiency or excess of any neuro-transmitter may cause bodily malfunctions. For example, a deficiency of serotonin may be linked to insomnia and severe depression. A deficiency of dopamine is linked to the tremors of Parkinson's disease, but an excess of dopamine may be involved in schizophrenia, which may also be caused by a deficiency of serotonin and acetylcholine. The body naturally produces painkiller neuro-transmitters known as enkephalins and endorphins, which operate to inhibit the transmission of pain signals across each synapse. These synaptic receptor sites may be blocked by analgesic drugs. The common feature of these substances is that they can mimic the neuro-transmitter in its ability to lock onto the surface of a synapse, but will not transmit a signal. Under normal conditions, opiate receptors are exposed to a certain level of enkephalins and endorphins. Opiates such as morphine or heroin bind to unoccupied enkephalin receptors, mimicking the pain suppressing effect of enkephalins. Repeated doses of heroin and morphine fill the enkaphalin receptors so that they cannot accept enkephalins, which then are no longer able to act as neuro-transmitters. When the supply of heroin and morphine is stopped, there is a period during which the pain receptors are no longer occupied by the opiate and the enkephalin production is insufficient to fill the void. This is the period of withdrawal symptoms.

The brain can process signals much faster than electronic computers, typically handling 10^{18} operations per second (as against 10^{10} for the fastest computers). Whereas animal brains consume around 5% of body energy expenditure, in humans the brain consumes 20%. The operation of the brain is still largely unknown, and the function of different areas has been derived from observed malfunctions due to strokes and haemorrhages, tumours and accidents. Additional information has also been gleaned by direct electrical stimulation of parts of the brain through an opening in the skull, with the subject conscious (the brain itself has no sensation of pain) and more recently by positron emission tomography.

The cerebrum forms the major part of the volume of the brain. It comprises two hemispheres linked by 300 million nerve fibres, known as the corpus callosum. The surface of the cerebrum is covered by a three millimetre thick layer of grey matter, the cerebral cortex, where the functions of memory, organisation, understanding, communication, evaluation and creativity are thought to reside. It has a total surface area of around 2,200 square centimetres. Between the brain stem and the cortex lie various structures, such as the hypothalamus and pituitary gland, that regulate body functions such as temperature, blood pressure, pulse rate, blood sugar, hormones, sexuality and electrolyte levels. The hypothalamus controls the pituitary gland, which is responsible for regulation of growth to adulthood and it in turn controls the function of the other endocrine glands in the body.

While neurons contain the same genetic information (DNA) in the cell nucleus as other cells, which is fixed at conception, they have the ability to store information based on sensory input, experience and learning. Thus individuality exists both genetically and experientially. Each neuron has many extensions, dendrites, through which signals are received and a single extension, the axon, along which signals are transmitted. Each extension ends in a synapse. Sensory neurons transmit information to the brain and motor neurons transmit signals to the muscles in response. Most of these signals travel through the spinal cord.

In addition there is the autonomic nervous system which relays information to the brain concerning organ functions, respiration, temperature, blood pressure, and comprises sympathetic and parasympathetic components. The former tends to increase the activity of glands and constrict involuntary muscles and blood vessels and the parasympathetic system opposes these changes. Working together, the two systems keep the organs and systems of the body working in balance but can adapt quickly to changes. These nerves not only pass through the spinal cord but also through ganglia on either side of the spine and the vagus nerves and operate without the conscious awareness of the subject.

One of the curious features of the brain and nervous system is the crossover of nerve connections in the brain stem, so that sensory information from the right half of the body communicates with the left hemisphere of the brain and vice versa. Where sight is concerned, the left half of each retina is connected to the left hemisphere of the brain and the right half to the right hemisphere. The sense of hearing is distributed in a similar complicated way between the auditory centres of each hemisphere. The two halves of the cerebrum reconstruct the sensory information and generate the appropriate motor response.

There are well defined regions within each cerebral hemisphere that receive sensory information and control motor functions of the body. In this respect the brain can be considered to be "hard-wired". When considering where knowledge and memory reside, there are no such clearly defined regions. Memory loss due to accidental damage to the brain has traditionally been the means by which those parts concerned with this function have been located. The accumulated evidence suggests that specific memories are distributed in several locations and loss or damage to any one does not erase the memory, but perhaps makes it hazier. It is known that short-term memory is associated with the hypothalamus but the location of long-term memory is still a mystery.

Although damage to brains and invasive stimulation have enabled scientists to glean much information about the location of various brain functions, it is in the area of psychology, the study of mentality and its dysfunctions that most progress has been made. Sigmund Freud (1856-1939) is the most significant figure, developing theories based on observation of the interpretation of dreams, the basis of emotions in the subconscious mind, sexuality and a study of the personality. Carl Jung (1875-1961) also developed psychoanalysis and studies of the unconscious mind, but unlike Freud he also delved into metaphysics, a study of the religious and spiritual aspects of psychology. Although Freud's contribution to this field is very significant for the present age, the study of the metaphysicial aspects of the human mind is more significant. It is in this area that this text will concentrate.

It is assumed by scientists that the mind and brain are one and the same. Yet there is abundant evidence that this is not the case, particularly in the area known as extrasensory perception or ESP. In general it concerns the acquisition of information that is not evident to the physical senses. The Society for Psychical Research has been engaged in studies of paranormal phenomena for almost 150 years, in a research programme that has caused the scientists great frustration because it seems that phenomena do not reproduce in the laboratory as they do in the outside world.

The most recent experiments to test for the existence of telepathy (mind to mind communication over a distance with no visible means of connection) involved two persons located in rooms some distance apart. The "sender" watched a series of computer generated images, in a random sequence, and mentally concentrated on each to send it to the second person, the "receiver". The "receiver" was blindfolded and soundproofed to minimise sensory distractions and dictated onto a tape recording a description of the images received. In a series of experiments, each involving four images in a random order, a tally of 25% success was expected due to chance alone, but actually there was repeatedly around 41% success. This was significant evidence of telepathy. The use of computer generated images and randomised sequencing eliminated any possibility of the experiment director contributing to telepathic results. However, when the "sender" was absent from his room but with the computer still generating images, the "receiver" continued to receive images with the same (unchanged) rate of success. This suggests that some other process was at work, in which the "receiver's" mind could perceive images displayed in a different location.

In much research animals and plants have been the subjects for experimentation. In the former USSR the offspring of a laboratory rabbit were taken in a submarine, underwater, at a distance of many hundreds of kilometres from the laboratory, in which the parent rabbit was wired to a polygraph or lie detector. The laboratory clock and submarine chronometer were synchronised. Each time a baby rabbit was killed, the parent registered a strong reaction on the polygraph. Evidently the mode of communication was able to cover a large distance and unlike radio waves, pass through sea water.

These two examples illustrate that there are unseen forms of communication between all life forms. We live our lives with the sensory input from our five senses dominating our consciousness. Yet it is evident that extrasensory perception is significant and operates within the mental region deemed "unconscious". Indeed, the subjective mind is capable of blocking input from the senses, as in daydreaming, emotions and imaginative activities.

Virtually all people can recall some instances of significant coincidences, *"déjà vu"* or awareness of events for which there is no normal sensory information. This also includes precognition, awareness of events before they happen. The abundance of these perceptions in the general population suggests that there are aspects of our mind that conventional psychology has chosen to ignore because they do not fit in with general theories. Carl Jung referred to this area as the "universal unconscious mind".

The holographic model of brain function

It is a curious feature of the brain that it has no sensation of pain. If the scalp and skull are anaesthetised, openings in the skull can be made in a fully conscious subject and electrodes introduced into the various parts of the brain, so that the reaction to stimulation can be observed.

It was Professor Wilder Penfield in the 1920s who discovered that electrical stimulation of the cerebral cortex of conscious subjects produced detailed recall of long forgotten memories. It therefore seemed that certain regions of the cortex held specific memories. Repeated stimulation of the same region always seemed to recall the same memory.

However, in experiments in the 1940s with rats, which had been trained to find their way through a maze, Professor Karl Lashley found that the rats still remembered the route even when up to 98% of the memory regions of their brains had been surgically removed (the motor centres were retained so that the rats could move through the maze). This suggested strongly that there are no specific memory centres, completely overturning Penfield's observations. This work was extended by Karl Pribram in the 1950s, in experiments where any part of the rat's cerebral cortex was removed, and yet the memory to navigate through the maze was retained. In accident victims where large sections of the cerebral cortex had to be removed, it was observed that detailed memories were not lost. Thus it was clear that memories were not held in any specific location and seemingly minute proportions of the cerebral cortex could recall the entire memory.

Pribram proposed the idea that the brain is analogous to a hologram in which all memories are encoded in all parts of the cerebral cortex. A hologram is a two dimensional interference pattern, such as is created on a photographic plate, when laser light reflected from an object interferes with a portion of the original laser beam. When the holographic plate is subsequently illuminated by laser light at the same frequency, a three dimensional image of the object is recreated. If the hologram is cut into many fragments, just one fragment, if so illuminated, will create the three dimensional image of the object. If different objects are projected at different frequencies and at various angles of incidence to create a hologram, three dimensional images of each object are recreated when the hologram is illuminated by light at the appropriate frequency and angle of incidence. Thus a single fragment of a hologram can hold many images. An estimate of the information storage capacity of a hologram is that a six square centimetre fragment of film could hold the same amount of information as fifty Bibles! By implication, if a two dimensional hologram can recreate a three dimensional image, the three dimensional brain must be operated upon by some agency that occupies an additional spatial dimension to recreate detailed recall of memories.

It was estimated by physicist and mathematician John von Neumann that a lifetime experience would correspond to 2.8×10^{20} bits of data stored in the memory of the brain. If distributed uniformly among 10^{11} neurons in the brain, this would correspond to the storage of over one billion bits of information per neuron. It has recently been suggested by Sandra Peria and Yuri Arshavsky of the University of California, Institute of Non-Linear Sciences that the nuclear DNA in neurons could provide the means for long-term storage of memories. Synaptic links between neurons and the chemical substances within them are constantly changing so that these could not form the basis of long-term memory storage. By contrast, DNA is stable. Most of the base sequence of human DNA seems not to be concerned with significant genetic information, so that human DNA differs from that of apes by only around 1.5% and of worms by 4%. It would therefore be conceivable that uncommitted parts of the DNA molecule could encode long-term memories. This would imply that the DNA of neurons was being continually changed, broken apart and reassembled using proteins that would be regarded as alien by the immune response system. However, the body's immune response system is not able to penetrate the membranes enclosing the brain, so that while this would leave the brain vulnerable to infection, it also would allow alien proteins to be created in the process shuffling the DNA base sequence for the purpose of storing memories. Thus each neuron could encode a billion memories in its DNA. However, damage to large parts of the brain does not destroy memories, so that specific memories are distributed across the cerebral cortex. Hence the DNA coding could be of an interference pattern as in a hologram, so that the entire memory can be retrieved from the stimulation of any part.

Another of Lashley's discoveries was that the visual centres are also holographic. After removing 90% of the rat's visual cortex (the part of the brain which receives and interprets what the eye sees), the rat could still perform tasks requiring complex visual skills. Similarly Pribram found that 98% of a cat's optic nerve could be severed without seriously impairing vision. Thus it appears there is no one-to-one correspondence between the image the eye perceives and the way it is represented in the brain. Further work measuring the electrical activity in the brains of monkeys while performing various visual tasks convinced Pribram that there was no correspondence between the perceived images and the storage in the brain nor any discernable pattern to the sequence that the implanted electrodes fired. Thus it seemed that the whole image was distributed in every part of the brain and visual sensory input is not hard-wired. Pribram published his findings in 1966 and has continued researching the holographic brain analogy since then.

Independent experimental support for the holographic model came from Paul Pietsch at the University of Indiana. He discovered that he could remove the brains of salamanders without killing them. He swapped the left and right hemispheres, sliced, shuffled and even minced the brains before replacing the remnants back in the heads of the salamanders and observed that their behaviour returned to normal.

When holography was first devised by Dennis Gabor in 1947 (and received a Nobel prize for the work in 1971), he used Fourier analysis to derive the principle. This is a mathematical procedure whereby complex patterns and waveforms can be reduced to a series of simple (sinusoidal) waves of various frequencies. This analysis enabled Gabor to convert a picture of an object into a blur of interference patterns on a holographic film and then recreate an image of the object from the hologram. During the 1960s and 70s, various researchers found that the human visual system operates as a frequency analyser. In 1979, neurophysiologists Russell and Karen DeValois found that brain cells in the visual cortex of subjects responded to images of chequerboard patterns by generating Fourier translations of the observed patterns. It proved conclusively that the brain operated as a Fourier analyser. These results were confirmed by many other laboratories around the world. It was soon realised that the ear was also a sound frequency analyser and that the sense of smell responded to osmic frequencies.

Further evidence that the brain acts as a Fourier analyser came from Russian scientist Nikolai Bernstein, who filmed dancers dressed in black against a black background, but with white dots on their elbows, knees and other joints. The developed film merely showed moving white dots. He used Fourier analysis of the motion of the dots and found that he could accurately predict their movement. Thus the dancers moved according to the directions from their brains which were evidently breaking down the motion into its Fourier components.

There have been other theories of brain function, but none can satisfactorily explain all facets of memory and brain to the extent of the holographic model. If the brain is indeed a three dimensional hologram, this raises important questions about the nature of the three dimensional world that we call reality. Just as it would be impossible for the residents of the hypothetical two dimensional world "Flatland" to conceive of a third dimension, so it is difficult for we residents of a three dimensional world to conceive of a fourth spatial dimension. Yet just such a concept may be necessary to reconcile the subatomic quantised world of strong and weak nuclear and electromagnetic forces with the cosmic macroscopic relativistic world of force due to gravity. Both electromagnetic forces and the force due to gravitational attraction obey the inverse square law, in which the intensity of the force decreases as the inverse square of the distance. However, gravity is so much weaker than electromagnetic force, as illustrated by the fact that a small bar magnet can lift an iron nail against the gravitational pull of the earth. Theoretical physicists now postulate that perhaps there are folds in the fabric of the three dimensional universe that make the effect of gravity appear so weak, in effect postulating the existence of a fourth spatial dimension. Many scientists react sceptically to this idea on the basis that if it can't be observed then it does not exist. It would be appropriate to point out that electromagnetic radiation beyond the visible spectrum and radioactivity could not be seen until the end of the nineteenth century and yet these formed a fundamental part of the development of twentieth century science and technology. Therefore twenty-first century physics may be concerned with the quest for the fourth spatial dimension!

The holographic model of the universe

The theory of a holographic universe was proposed by the eminent physicist David Bohm in 1957 while he was professor of physics at Princeton University. It was Bohm's research with plasmas at the Berkeley Radiation Research Laboratory that convinced him that subatomic matter was somehow interconnected. A plasma is considered to be the fourth state of matter (solids, liquids and gases being the other three), in which the electrons are completely stripped from atoms, which then exist as nuclei, and is usually at a high temperature and contained by electric and magnetic fields. Bohm observed that a plasma tended to behave as an organised interconnected whole rather than as a vast collection of independent electrons and nuclei, moving randomly. Subsequent studies of electrons in metals confirmed his observation of seemingly highly organised overall effects. He called these collective movements "plasmons".

Bohm and Einstein had discussed the strange indeterminacy of matter at the atomic level predicted by quantum physics (as proposed by Niels Bohr) during the early 1950s. In particular it was Bohr's assertion that the properties of matter at the atomic and subatomic level could only be defined when they were being observed and may be different at all other times. If the act of observation actually helped create those properties, which otherwise do not exist, it implied that subatomic particles were interconnected in a manner unacceptable to Einstein. He published a paper jointly with Boris Podolsky and Nathan Rosen in 1935 entitled "Can quantum mechanical description of physical reality be considered complete?", in which a twin photon experiment was proposed to test the interconnectedness of matter. The technology of the time did not allow such an experiment to be performed.

At the beginning of this chapter the technique of positron emission tomography is described as a method of producing physiological images of the brain. The two gamma rays produced when a positron annihilates with an electron travel in opposite directions, each at the speed of light. According to quantum physics, no matter how far apart these photons travel, when they are measured, they will have identical polarisation at the same instant of time. This would require faster than light communication between them. However, if the two photons were regarded as interconnected via a fourth spatial dimension from the moment of their creation, faster than light communication would not be necessary.

In 1982 experimental verification of the interconnectedness of matter was observed at the University of Geneva by Alain Aspect, Jean Dalibard and Gerard Roger. A crystal containing calcium was illuminated with a laser and produced two light photons travelling in opposite directions. These photons were passed through several kilometers of optic fibres, both of which terminated in a polarizer and detector. Only photons with the same polarization would reach the detectors, which were linked by fast electronics. Both photons were detected simultaneouly, so were identically polarized. This showed that the predictions of quantum theory were correct and that the pair of photons were linked regardless of their separation. If faster than light communication is not possible, as Einstein asserts, the link between them may be via a fourth spatial dimension.

The theories of Karl Pribram and David Bohm suggest that our brains construct objective reality by interpreting frequencies that are ultimately projections from another dimension. The brain is a hologram enfolded in a holographic universe.

The holographic model applied to psychology

It was Carl Jung who observed that certain subjective experiences among his patients had objective value, and often concerned past events of which the subject could have had no conscious knowledge. It was this observation that led Jung to propose the existence of the universal unconscious mind. In effect, anyone could tap into a vast pool of knowledge under certain circumstances which lay beyond their physical senses and the memories of their own life experience.

It was Montague Ullman, the founder of the Dream Laboratory at the Maimonides Medical Centre in Brooklyn, New York, who concluded that all people were interconnected within a holographic order. He had conducted many ESP and dream experiments which showed considerable evidence that people communicated in ways previously not considered. Since we all spend between a quarter and a third of our lives asleep, this part of our lives may be more significant than the period that we spend awake, in an environment dominated by our five physical senses. One of the most famous instances was that of Emmanuel Swedenborg who dreamed of a great fire in a city some distance away from where he was and on waking found that the fire had indeed occurred. The dreams often contain great wisdom and truth, beyond the understanding of the dreamer.

Ullman's study of psychosis showed considerable evidence of holographic ideas. The psychotics are unable to order their experiences rationally so are only able to recall a distorted version. Schizophrenics are unable to relate the correct sequence of events and manic depressives' recall of their experiences are chaotic.

Another area of research is into lucid dreams, where the dreamer is able to control the course of events in the dream, which

41

nevertheless acquires a realism equivalent to the physical world. It was physicist Fred Alan Wolf who in 1987 outlined the theory that holograms produce two images, a virtual image on one side where light beams are diverging and a real image on the other where light converges to a focus. He believed that all dreams are internal holograms producing virtual images but he likened the lucid dream to the real image.

The most influential investigator in this area is Professor Stanislav Grof, of the Maryland Psychiatric Research Center and John Hopkins University School of Medicine, who spent over thirty years studying non-ordinary states of consciousness. While at the Psychiatric Research Institute in Prague, he investigated the therapeutic value of lysergic acid diethylamide, LSD. The results were striking. It seemed that the repeated treatment with the drug gave progressively deeper access to the patient's unconscious mind, shortening the time necessary for the treatment of many disorders. Many experiences recalled were found to relate to other people who lived in other times and other cultures, which lay beyond the life experience of the subject. Some experiences even extended to animal life forms. Subsequent research validated many of these accounts. Grof described these as transpersonal experiences.

Grof and his colleagues extended his work with LSD to normal volunteers, conducting over 3,000 sessions, each lasting several hours. The results convinced him that the models of psychology inherited from Freud and Jung were inadequate and incomplete, that there was a much greater reality beyond the conscious mind that was accessible under the influence of LSD. One instance was of a young man who encountered another presence during his experience, who telepathically communicated his name, address and telephone number. When the professor dialled the number, he found that he had called the parents of a son who had died just three weeks previously, and that the name and address given were correct. Other experiences gave uncannily accurate precognition of events. Thus it seems that the mind can transcend the barriers of both time (past, present and future) and space, operating in the fourth dimension.

Grof and his wife developed a simple technique without the use of drugs to induce the same kind of non-ordinary state of consciousness, in the form of physical and breathing exercises, music and massage. They termed these non-ordinary states holotropic, in which it is possible to access the holographic labyrinth that connects all aspects of existence.

The condition known as multiple personality disorder, a fragmentation of the psyche, is known to arise as the result of childhood trauma, as though the trauma is reduced by being shared between different personalities. Whereas normal individuals show a consistent brain wave pattern even in extreme states of emotion, each personality manifest in the multiple personality disorder exhibits a different brain wave pattern. These patterns are a property of the whole brain, and imply that there is a switching from one hologram to another when the personality changes. Some individuals with this disorder can exhibit dozens of personalities, rapidly switching from one to the next.

An experience common to most people are meaningful coincidences or synchronicities. Often these occurrences relate subjective experiences to external events. According to Bohm, the apparent separateness of consciousness and matter is an illusion. If there is no separation between mind and matter in reality, the coincidences may actually be found in the same hologram. Synchronicities may actually be flaws in the fabric of reality, that there is no real division between the physical world and our inner psychological reality. This conflicts with the common sense notion that subjective and objective reality are very much separate. It implies that objective reality may be a form of dreaming, in which the five physical senses create the illusion.

Mind control of the body

The autonomic nervous system controls the function of the body and organs via the sympathetic and parasympathetic nervous systems, operating in opposition to each other. This operates without conscious awareness until the body systems become out of balance.

The placebo effect is a well known factor in drug research, and must be eliminated in order to evaluate the effectiveness and efficacy of the new medication. Prior to the twentieth century, it can be claimed that the placebo effect accounted for most of the benefit derived from remedies prescribed by the medical profession.

A placebo is any medical treatment that has no specific action on the body but is given to humour the patient or as a control in a double blind experiment. In such experiments, neither the researcher nor the subjects being tested know who received the drug and who received the placebo. It is now known that on average 35% of all people who receive the placebo will derive significant benefit from it. In the surgical treatment of angina pectoris, in an experiment, some patients who were just cut open and then stitched up again derived as much benefit as those who received the normal surgery. In the treatment of migraine headaches, allergies, fevers, the common cold, acne, asthma, warts, various kinds of pain, nausea and seasickness, peptic ulcers, psychiatric syndromes such as depression and anxiety, rheumatoid and degenerative arthritis, diabetes, radiation sickness, Parkinsonism, multiple schlerosis and various cancers, the placebo effect is very significant. It shows that the mind is very effective in controlling the body via the autonomic nervous system. Conversely the mind can cause illness by creating imbalances in the body.

The placebo effect can operate in whole populations. In an

experiment where two groups of ten people were taking amphetamines or barbiturates, when one of the ten in each group was prescribed the stimulant and the other nine the tranquilliser, and vice versa in the other group, the individual receiving different medication from the others nevertheless experienced the same effect as the other nine in the same group.

In the USA the ability of aspirin to prevent heart attacks has been promoted extensively in advertising. Yet there is no evidence of this benefit in a six-year trial of aspirin in Britain. Whenever a new drug appears on the market there is a surge in the beneficial response of people to whom it is prescribed but this falls back as people become accustomed to taking it. Similarly when a placebo is substituted for a drug, there is a beneficial reaction, and where the side effects of the real drug are known, the people who received the placebo exhibit the same side effects. The effectiveness of placebos is so significant that it can be asked what is the true effectiveness of many drugs prescribed today.

Perhaps the most striking example of the placebo effect lies in the treatment of people suffering from the multiple personality disorder. In this condition, each personality not only exhibits a completely different brain wave pattern, but different physical attributes and ailments, such as short-sightedness, left and right handedness and even eye colour. The conditions of epilepsy, diabetes, colour blindness, scars and burns appear and disappear with the change of personality. The response to drugs changes similarly, so that one personality who became drunk after an intake of alcoholic beverage is followed by another who is completely sober. Tumours have also been known to appear and disappear in multiple personalities. It has been observed that these people age less quickly, heal more rapidly and exhibit multiple talents, such as the ability to work on several (mental) tasks simultaneously.

The demand for complementary and alternative therapies today illustrates the shortcomings of conventional medicine. In evaluating the efficacy and effectiveness of any drug or medicine the placebo effect must be eliminated. In order to evaluate the effectiveness of any complementary or alternative therapy, similar criteria need to be applied. However, in the case of herbal remedies, where the effect is the result of several chemical agents operating in combination, the experimental method used to evaluate a single substance (drug) may not be appropriate although such a trial would be appropriate to evaluate homeopathy. In the case of acupuncture, spiritual healing, reflexology, chiropractic and osteopathy, performing a double blind trial is impossible.

Alternative and complementary therapies have a common philosophy that mind and body are linked, and that the body is a network of systems held in balance. Disease is therefore an imbalance in the body, where the normal processes of self-regulation break down. It is an assumption of alternative and complementary therapies that the body can "learn" how to regulate itself more effectively and the various therapies are therefore aimed not at a specific cure for symptoms as in much conventional medicine but to disturb the system back into balance. In effect the intelligent body is made to "relearn" so that it can self-regulate more effectively.

The body's natural ability to control pain by production of endorphins was shown in a recent study by Fabrizio Benedetti of Turin University in which saline was subsituted for morphine and the patient still felt pain relief. When the drug naloxone was added to the saline placebo, which acts to inhibit the production of natural endorphins, the patient felt no pain relief. Thus brain imaging studies are presently ongoing to locate the source of placebo analgesia. Without doubt, the placebo effect forms a large part of alternative and complementary therapies, but it would be misleading to dismiss these therapies as being only just such an effect.

It has now been found that some herbs, containing several active agents are more potent than alapathic drugs. The conventional drug has been developed as a specific biochemical agent, a magic bullet to treat a specific condition. Thus herbs may be a source of new medicines, in which the actions of the various ingredients together are more potent while counteracting the side effects that often are associated with the conventional drug. For example, garlic can be used as an antiseptic, and to treat high blood pressure and high cholesterol levels; ginseng as a tonic to reduce stress and ageing, stimulate immune functions and boost physical and sexual performance; kava kava as a sedative and tranquiliser; echinacea to treat wounds, burns and respiratory infections including the common cold; ginkgo for cognitive problems, improving concentration, amnesia, mild dementia, tinnitus and vertigo, also macular degeneration and arterial disease; St John's wort for moderate depression and saw palmetto as a therapy for benign enlargement of the prostate gland. In many instances, the combined effect of the chemical ingredients is greater than if each were given separately. For some, such as St John's wort, the effect is clearly beyond that of a placebo.

So far only a limited analysis of the chemical agents in herbs has been completed. The active ingredient of kava kava is kavapyrones, which has been isolated and found to be a tranquilliser. Ginkgo has been found to contain two active agents: flavonoids, which act as antioxidants and ginkgoloids which inhibit blood clotting. St John's wort contains more than two dozen active ingredients, and has side effects common to many antidepressants. It is ineffective against severe depression. In their action, herbs seem to be better than the sum of their active constituents, which probably act in a complementary fashion, minimising side effects from each other.

In Chinese medicine, acupuncture is considered to release the opposing forces of Yin and Yang, thereby restoring the balance between them so that the life energy Qi can flow. The meridians along which this flow occurs are located under the skin and form complete circuits around the body. Western science has found that inserting acupuncture needles stimulates the production of endorphins. Injecting naloxone inhibits the production of endorphins so that no pain relief occurs. Apart from pain relief, acupuncture has been found to be effective in treating nausea caused by anaesthetics and chemotherapy for cancer; also used in conjunction with conventional therapies it is effective in treating addictions, headaches, menstrual cramps, tennis elbow, muscular pain, osteoarthritis, lower back pain, carpal tunnel syndrome and asthma and assists with rehabilitation after strokes. Studies have shown that it is ineffective for stopping smoking, for Parkinson's disease and tinnitus (ringing in the ears). Acupuncture has few side effects provided precautions are taken to avoid infection from the insertion of needles.

The effect of acupuncture is apparently improved when needles are twisted periodically (the Oriental method) or connected to an alternating electric power source (the Western method). It has been shown that a low frequency of 2 Hz (cycles per second) causes the release of enkephalins in the spinal cord and beta-endorphins in the mid-brain and a higher frequency of 100 Hz causes the release of dynorphin in the spinal cord. It has been found to be effective in treating heroin addicts, when the Hoku point between the thumb and forefinger is needled for thirty minutes per day for two weeks and 100 Hz electrical stimulation applied. This relieves nausea as dynorphins are released. Thereafter the chronic craving is relieved by 2 Hz stimulation at this point causing endorphins to be released which mimic the action of morphine. However these observations require confirmation. It may be that a patient's genetic make-up affects their response to acupuncture and may explain the variable results. Some individuals may naturally produce chemicals in their bodies that block the action of endorphins and negate the pain-killing effect of acupuncture.

Traditional Chinese medicine uses detailed maps of the meridians and acupuncture points, many of which have specific target regions. Recent work with brain scanning suggests that it does indeed matter which acupuncture points are used, but that the Chinese meridian system was merely their way of mapping the acupuncture points at a time when the nervous system was not understood. Since placebos can also cause the release of endorphins in the brain and nervous system, it is yet to be shown that acupuncture can have an effect beyond that of a placebo. The effectiveness of acupuncture beyond the placebo effect may depend critically on the choice of points and the type of (electrical) stimulation applied at these points. Much research remains to be done. In Oriental medicine, acupuncture was practiced in conjunction with herbal medicine and its true effectiveness in the West may lie in restoring its Eastern context.

Homeopathy challenges conventional Western medicine by stating that more dilute solutions of the active ingredients are more potent. The degree of dilution employed in homeopathic medicine is such that not one molecule of the active agent would be present in the solution, which in effect is just water. The remedy resembles vaccination in that the substance which cause the symptoms it is desired to treat triggers a healing response in the body. This is based on the principle laid down by homeopathy's founder, Samuel Hahnemann, at the end of the eighteenth century, that "like cures like". This principle was the result of the observation that quinine, used to treat malaria, actually produced malaria-like symptoms in healthy subjects. Hahnemann experimented with other drugs and found that the therapeutic effect increased as he diluted them.

In practice a solution of the active substance in ethanol is diluted between six and thirty times as one part in 100 of an ethanol-water mixture, and at each dilution the solution is shaken vigorously or "succussed". This degree of dilution would result in a sample containing not one molecule of the active substance, in which case the therapeutic effect is due to the water itself. This implies that the water must have a memory of the active ingredient, which may be implanted in the water by the vigorous succussing process at each dilution. (Could this relate to the water that is "energised" by a healer to promote more rapid plant growth?)

Recent statistical trials of homeopathic remedies have concluded that they do have an effect beyond that expected of a placebo. Histamine at homeopathic dilutions was shown to suppress the activity of basophils, white blood cells which naturally produce histamine to combat infection and cause inflammation. Since this could not be explained by conventional chemical science, an alternative explanation is being sought, perhaps suggesting that water itself may have a memory!

Traditional Chinese medicine has at its core the concept of life energy or Qi (pronounced chi). Illness occurs when the flow of this energy in the body is interrupted, causing an imbalance. Thus all therapies are designed to remove the interruption and promote normal flow of Qi. This may be the action of spiritual healers, of various kinds, who by laying hands on the patient, or placing their hands in close proximity to the patient without touching, are able to supply some form of life energy. Many clairvoyants are able to see energy fields or auras around patients, which can provide diagnostic information of any illness afflicting them, perhaps even in advance of physical symptoms manifesting.

Dr Walter Kilner, a physician at St Thomas Hospital, London, in 1911 developed some spectacles with filtered lenses which enabled him to see the auric emanations around his patients, and from this carry out medical diagnosis. This was followed up by Cambridge biologist Oscar Bagnall who used specialised spectacles with hollowed lenses, which when filled with freshly-prepared solutions of the coal tar dye dicyanin or pinacyanol dissolved in triethanolamine, enabled him to see the human energy field and make certain observations. He described the aura as comprising two layers, the inner one being brighter and well defined and the outer much hazier. The aura seemed to be attracted to a magnet held close to the skin and extended furthest from the body at its extremities such as the finger and nose. The effect of the dye was probably that of a wavelength shifter, making visible emanations

D

that would be found in the near ultraviolet or near infrared regions of the electromagnetic spectrum. Unfortunately the dye was only effective for a period of around half an hour, so that the device was not practical for routine diagnostic procedures. However, in 1939, an accidental exposure to high voltages used in X-ray equipment led Semyan Kirlian to develop a high frequency electrostatic imaging device that produces images on film of the energy field around leaves and human extremities such as fingers. These energy fields indicate the state of health of the subject. In the case of a leaf which had been partly cut away, the image of the missing part was still evident. The fingers of people who were under the influence of alcohol or drugs showed characteristic emanations, but most striking were the emanations around the fingers of a healing medium, which exhibited bright flares. Corona discharges around objects placed in high electric fields is well known but the patterns observed here included information about the state of health of the subject or sample.

It should not be surprising that there are energy fields surrounding living tissues. Any flow of electrons in a wire produces electromagnetic waves, and conversely electromagnetic waves produce a flow of electrons in a wire. Therefore electrochemical processes in tissues would be expected to produce emissions in some part of the electromagnetic spectrum. Conversely electromagnetic waves could induce changes in electrochemical processes. The most common instance of this is photosynthesis, where light photons with energy around four electron volts are sufficient to promote the synthesis of carbohydrates from carbon dioxide and water in conjunction with the chlorophyll molecule. Photons of higher energy (such as ultraviolet radiation) would destroy vital chemical bonds and therefore be detrimental to life on this planet. However, radiations of lower energy can change the shape of molecules and thereby drastically affect their biological function. It may be that the energy from a healer as well as the body's own energy field can influence the rate of biochemical processes in the body, changing the balance point between opposing reactions.

In studying the chemical processes in a cell nucleus, the synthesis of polypeptides from twenty amino acids involves not just joining molecules together in the correct sequence, but subsequent bending of the molecule into a secondary structure which gives the three dimensional shape to the molecule. This in turn is twisted into a tertiary structure which enables the polypeptide to construct a protein molecule. Proteins seem to be smart in the sense that they twist correctly to adopt the shape necessary to perform their function within the cell. There are many possibilities for incorrect twists and structures to occur but they seldom do, and when this does occur, other proteins intervene to repair the error. Chemical thermodynamics would naturally lead to a breakdown of this highly ordered process, causing an increased degree of disorder (increase of entropy) which does indeed occur at the death of the cell or whole organism. The combustion of glucose and the conversion of adenosine triphosphate fuel the synthesis of proteins and the differences of energy between the correct and incorrect molecular shape is tiny. Thus it could be that the energy field of the organism may control the correct choice of the direction that the synthesis of each protein molecule takes. If this is proven to be true, it has profound implications for our understanding of biological mechanisms, not just in the human body but generally in nature.

Professor Valerie Hunt of the University College of Los Angeles has made significant measurements of the human energy field. Routine measurements of electrical activity in muscles, electromyograms or EMGs, have revealed a high frequency but low amplitude component, particularly in areas of the body corresponding to the "chakras" or vortices that are known to exist in the energy body surrounding the physical body. This is clearly different from the normal electrical activity of the brain, heart and muscles. The electrical activity of the brain, as recorded on an electroencephalograph (EEG), is between 0 and 100 Hz (cycles per second) with most occurring below 30 Hz, which is arbitrarily divided into four bands labelled delta (1 to 4 Hz), theta (4 to 8 Hz), alpha (8 to 13 Hz) and beta (13 to 30 Hz). Beta waves correspond to the normal waking state, alpha waves denote a state of relaxed awareness, theta waves a dreamy or drowsy mental state and delta waves emanate from the sleeping brain. Muscle frequencies go up to 225 Hz and heart frequencies (recorded by an electrocardiogram or ECG) go up to around 250 Hz, but above this there are no signals normally connected with biological activity. Hunt's observation of small signals with frequencies from 100 Hz to above 1.6 kHz in the vicinity of body chakras was therefore very significant. It became more significant when the signals were analysed for patterns in an otherwise random emission (seeking to find regularities in apparent chaos). The results of the chaos analysis showed no patterns in the EEG and ECG signals and the normal lower frequency EMG signals, but the high frequencies in the EMG showed an "extremely dynamic" system of very highly ordered but non-repeating patterns. If the subjects on whom the measurements were made were known to be mystics, very high frequencies were observed, up to 200 kHz, for which the EMG apparatus had to be modified in order to observe these signals (EMG analysers normally have an upper frequency limit of 20 kHz). More recent measurements by others have revealed similar chaos patterns in EEG measurements of the brain. Hunt's measurements were taken with a single electrode and three to four seconds of data were sufficient to yield a chaos pattern containing information which was far more complex and dynamic than that of the brain. This may be the first objective observation of an energy field that could be responsible for directing biological processes at a molecular level. Psychics have made observations of the human aura and described artefacts that have preceded the onset of illness, often by several weeks and months. Thus research into this area could lead to new and potent forms of medical diagnosis and treatment.

The power of the mind can even change genetic predisposition to certain illnesses and there is evidence that changes in cellular DNA can result. Michael Talbot cites an example in the "Holographic Universe" where the symptoms of a sufferer from Brocq's disease, a genetically caused hardening of the skin which results in cracking and bleeding, who responded successfully to hypnotherapy. This has significant implications for all sufferers from genetically inherited conditions such as cystic fibrosis. If the mind can in some way alter the electrical fields in cells associated with the nuclear DNA, so that defective genes may correct themselves, new mental therapies may be found that circumvent the need for genetic engineering.

The deoxyribonucleic acid (DNA) double helix comprises two helically intertwined chains, each comprising repeating ribose-phosphate groups and linked by adenine (A) and thymine (T) or cytosine (C) and guanine (G) molecules. It is the sequence of the AT and CG links that determine the genetic code. Since these may be reversed, (TA) and (GC), there are four possible combinations for this coding system. When compared to the binary coding system used by computers, this squares the number of permutations.

The DNA helix is assembled using the RNA template and the four molecules, deoxyadenosine (A), deoxythymidine (T), deoxycytidine (C) and deoxyguanosine (G). The RNA template itself is replicated so that the genetic code can be transmitted. It is well known that ionising radiation can damage the DNA double helix, breaking at least one strand of the helix. The cell endeavours to repair the break before proceeding with the process of cell division. If both strands of the double helix are broken, repair is impossible and the cell loses the ability to reproduce. This is the basis of radiation therapy for cancer. When repair of a single strand is incorrect, the result is a genetic mutation. This occurs as the process of ageing. At the molecular level, the relative positioning of molecules and the electrical charges upon them determine what combinations can occur. The energy difference between a correct and incorrect sequence is very small, and small changes in an electromagnetic field could influence the course of synthesis of the RNA and DNA molecules. When one considers that the activity of the mind can influence the electromagnetic field around the body, it is conceivable that genetic diseases are amenable to mind control, such as in a state of hypnosis.

There are many examples of mind over matter, but perhaps the most striking was Marin Dajo, who gave stage performances in which he was stabbed and run through with a fencing rapier, with no apparent ill effects. While so impaled he was examined and X-rayed by physicians, who certified that the blade did indeed pass through his abdomen, but when withdrawn, only faint red marks showed the point of entry and exit of the blade, which soon disappeared. Vital organs were pierced which would normally have had serious consequences. Evidently Dajo's degree of mind control over his body was able to cause rapid healing of the wounds and prevent sepsis from occurring, perhaps by rapid stimulation of the immune response system.

The ability of certain individuals to withstand high temperatures that would normally incinerate and vaporize human tissue has been chronicled through history. Aside from firewalkers who can traverse barefoot across glowing embers, there have been individuals who could handle incandescent metal, allow molten lead shot to solidify in the mouth and various ecstatic Pentecostalists who could endure holding their hands in an oxyacetylene flame without harm. This implies that the minds of the individuals concerned could create an invisible barrier between the body and the high temperature source.

A holographic interpretation of this would be that the three-dimensional world is not reality but a construction of the mind and that these individuals could displace their bodies into a different dimension. Thus Sai Baba, the Indian mystic, can create "apports" out of thin air, in full public view, in such abundance that it is a routine occurrence. Objects being created in this manner must have a source, and another dimension of existence may be the explanation. This may also be the explanation for the occurrence of stigmata in certain devout individuals, some later canonized by the Catholic Church. One such person was Theresa Neumann of Regensburg, who for the last thirty-five years of her life neither ate nor drank anything. She was evidently able to materialize all the bodily nutrition and water she needed as well as replace blood lost from the stigmata, without loss of weight.

Another example of mind over matter is illustrated by Oskar Esterbany, a Hungarian army officer who was also a well established healing medium. In one experiment, rats were given a 2.5cm incision in the skin of their backs. They were then divided into three equal groups. The rats of the first group each received five minutes "healing" each day from the army officer, who held his hands in close proximity. The rats of the second group were placed in a warm environment (at 37 degrees C) for the same period each day to mimic the heat of the healer's hands. The third group received no treatment. It was observed that the skin wound in each rat of the first group healed in one third of the time that the wounds in the other two groups of rats healed, in which the rate of healing was the same. The same healing medium was also required to give "healing" to a group of plants, which responded with more rapid growth than untreated plants of the same kind. To try to trace the cause of the accelerated growth, the healer was subsequently just permitted to give healing to the water used to irrigate the plants each day, with a control group irrigated with untreated water. Again, the plants receiving the "healed" water showed accelerated growth over the control group. This example illustrates the ability of the mind to administer some form of "life energy" that both promotes growth and accelerates healing. This ability even seems to affect the composition of water in a subtle fashion, which makes up 73% of the mass of the lean human body (excluding fat which is anhydrous).

All chemistry and biochemistry operates on reactions between molecules, in which electrical forces of attraction operate. In the case of enzymes, which promote most of the chemistry of the human body without being changed themselves, electrical charges on certain parts of the molecule cause it to attach to a matching part of another molecule. If a subtle change occurs in the distribution of electrical charges on the molecule or the tertiary structure (shape) of the molecules concerned, the speed of reaction will be changed very significantly, in most cases inhibited but occasionally accelerated. Where competing reactions are occurring in opposition to each other to create a balance, the net effect is that the balance is changed. Perhaps the action of the "life energy" from a healer operates at this level, even to the extent of producing subtle changes in the structure of water molecules, which are essential to all metabolic processes.

Water is the substance common to all metabolic processes in nature. Two hydrogen atoms bonded to an oxygen atom should be in gaseous form at normal body temperatures except that hydrogen bonding to oxygen atoms of adjacent molecules creates greater cohesion so that water is the familiar liquid. This ability of hydrogen to bond with certain electronegative elements such as oxygen, chlorine and fluorine has a fundamental importance to the existence of life. Not only water molecules remain loosely bound together (until the temperature is raised to 100 degrees centigrade, the boiling point) but the two intertwined DNA helices are similarly linked, in this case by sharing hydrogen between nitrogen and oxygen atoms. Thus the two strands of the DNA double helix can be "unzipped" with a minimum expenditure of energy, which occurs during the process of cell division, mitosis. Thus complementary sequences are transferred to each daughter cell nucleus which acts as a template for synthesis of the other strand.

If a healer can change the structure of water so that it promotes accelerated growth in plants that are irrigated with it, and homeopathic substances can leave an imprint in water of the original homeopathic substance, that is "potentised" by several dilutions with percussive shaking after each dilution, we have a clue as to how subtle influences can have a profound effect on health and wellbeing. The hydrogen bond between adjacent water molecules is weak and could be influenced by very small changes of energy as may be created in the energy body surrounding the physical body. This energy body is strongly influenced by the mind, and Valery Hunt's observation of high frequency components in the EMG signals in the vicinity of body "chakras" seems to provide evidence for this. This creates the possibility of employing biofeedback techniques to correct imbalances in the energy body which otherwise would eventually manifest themselves as illness.

Music can be a power for healing. We are very susceptible to influence from music since it is the only art form that bypasses the intellectual filter. At frequencies of just over 1 Hz (72 cycles per minute) there is a soothing influence since this corresponds to the mother's heartbeat that the foetus experiences when in the womb. At frequencies of around 7 Hz, the awake subject rapidly becomes excited and enraged, corresponding to the EEG theta band superimposed on the normal waking (beta band) state. Stroboscopic lighting in this frequency range can be dangerous, causing fits in epileptics, the onset of violence and an increased risk of car accidents where sunlight flickers between roadside trees. The EEG pattern of people subjected to this visual stimulus rapidly synchronises with it. A flicker of 25 Hz has an attractive hypnotic effect, which corresponds to the frame frequency of television and cinema, which probably accounts for the popularity of these media. Harmonising notes sound pleasing but discords, particularly those which produce a beat frequency around 7 Hz, are unpleasant. It has been observed that harmonising music can promote the growth of plants, boost milk and egg yields when played to poultry and cattle, and improve mood and induce mental relaxation in the human listener.

The alpha EEG frequency band (8 to 13 Hz) is associated with meditation, extrasensory perception and telepathy, in both the sender and receiver. The theta band (4 to 7 Hz) superimposed on the beta band (13 to 30 Hz) is the predominant emission from subjects performing psychokinesis. This mental state corresponds to a mood of suppressed rage, with elevated blood pressure, reduced skin resistance and increased perspiration. The most famous example of psychokinesis is the ability to bend cutlery and keys that thousands of people discovered while watching Uri Geller perform this on television. It is noteworthy that this state of mind was induced in so many people through the hypnotic medium of television.

Many years ago I worked with a trance healing medium, who was "controlled" by an African whilst healing. Initially the African entity spoke little English but over time (years) his command of the language improved. In this state he had "X-ray" vision of the patient and could diagnose conditions not evident to the normal person. One patient presented for healing for his eyes, but the entranced healer immediately observed a badly healed compound fracture of the right femur, which had been sustained several years earlier in a car accident. The patient walked normally so there was no external evidence of his earlier injury.

One of the most famous examples of mind over matter, that is well attested in the literature and that was subject to a preliminary scientific evaluation, is the work of the Brazilian psychic surgeon Jose de Freitas, also known as Arigo. For many years until his untimely death in 1971 in a car accident he had practised various forms of surgery without disinfection of his hands and operating knife nor with his patients anaesthetised. Each surgical procedure lasted less than one minute (which would have taken at least one hour with conventional surgery) and approximately seventy patients were seen by him during each hour of his clinic. Patients felt no pain during the procedures, often involving surgery on the eyes, and no instances of postoperative sepsis were reported. His success rating was at least comparable to that of any conventional surgeon, but because of his speed of working, the number of people treated was phenomenal, in excess of three hundred per day. When operating on patients he was entranced and evidently controlled by a German surgeon who could converse in both German and Portuguese (Arigo himself had no knowledge of German). The medications he prescribed were an odd combination of obsolete, current and newly marketed drugs (the latter often not available in Brazil at the time) whose effect, though beneficial to the patient's condition, was not as expert pharmacologists would have predicted. Arigo was the product of a culture, though nominally Catholic, essentially spiritist in nature and there are many others who exhibit similar gifts, but are not as willing to submit to rigorous scientific investigation.

More recently on the Philippine island of Luzon, a similar phenomenon has manifest in the form of psychic surgeons who appeared to be able to perform invasive operations with just their hands, without anaesthesia or disinfection. This is again the result of a spiritist culture within a nominally Catholic country.

These operations have a dramatic appeal since they produce quantities of blood and tissue in the vicinity of the healer's hands.

Samples taken of the blood and tissues for laboratory analysis give mixed results, suggesting in some instances that the tissue was of animal origin, but otherwise the blood and tissue matched that of the patient. The operations were performed publicly, taking often no more than five minutes, and were closely watched by observers for any sleight of hand, which in most cases seemed impossible. The healers themselves exhibited alpha brain waves when operating, as if in a trance state, and none had the necessary medical knowledge of a doctor.

These few examples illustrate that the mind is not just able to control the body in hitherto unsuspected ways but can also influence plants, animals and most other humans. The distinction between subjective (internal thoughts, feelings and emotions) and objective reality becomes vague within the context of these abilities. The increasing incidence of cancer in Western society is an example of how mental stress can detrimentally affect bodily health by undermining the operation of the immune response system.

Mind without the body

Modern physics has revealed that matter is just condensed energy. The materials from which our bodies and the physical universe is composed, and of which we are aware through our physical senses, is composed of mostly empty space with minute particles held together by force fields. The world of the atom is very strange, bearing little resemblance to the everyday physical world. The particles themselves, though composing the mass of the objects which they comprise, are not solid particles but intense energy fields which can be broken into even smaller constituents. Therefore if matter is condensed energy, what is mind? If mind is not the brain, it may be able to exist independently of the brain.

One of the most common mysteries is the purpose of sleep. We spend up to one third of our lives in sleep, which seems to be necessary not to relax the body but to relax the mind. Newly-born babies sleep nearly all the time, during which the interconnections of their brains are being formed, as the result of their experiences while awake. It is as though the mind suffers stress operating a physical body through the brain and needs periods of rest from the process. For young babies, this is a new experience and the process is more stressful and requires longer periods of rest. Dreaming seems to be an essential part of this process of mental recuperation and it has been found to be accompanied by rapid eye movements. When subjects of sleep experiments are deprived of dreaming sleep, they suffer short-term memory loss, loss of concentration, and when allowed to sleep immediately enter the dreaming phase for a prolonged period. The physiological responses of the body during dreaming seem quite stressful, which raised heart rate and blood pressure to high levels but without evident harm to the body.

It has been the contention of most religions of the world that the mind or spirit survives physical death, and that the mind therefore can exist independently of the body. In the Hague, a Dr Zaalberg Van Zeist weighed a dying patient and observed a sudden loss of weight of exactly 69.5 grams at the moment of clinical death. A similar test in England by a Dr Duncan McDougal yielded a similar value of 2.43 ounces (approximately 70 grams). One presumes these measurements were taken with instruments of sufficient sensitivity for the change of weight to be significant. Bearing in mind that death is a process rather than an event, it would be most useful if the loss of mass could be correlated with some other physiological event such as cessation of electrical activity in the brain stem. Clairvoyants claim to be able to observe the spirit mind leaving the body as a mass of fog rising over the deathbed. However, due to modern medical science, people have been revived from conditions that would otherwise have been fatal. They report consistently that they find themselves floating above the body, with a feeling of wellbeing and a lack of concern about their body. They are able to observe accurately the medical procedures carried out on their body and having passed through the walls and roof of the hospital can also observe the physical environment. Many subjects recounting near death experiences recall entering a tunnel with light at the far end (analogous to the birth canal?) at the end of which they encounter splendid beings of light and family members who have died previously. In many instances, when told that their time was not yet due, they returned reluctantly and regained physical consciousness in their physical body. It would be interesting to observe a change of body weight during such a near death experience, though of course the medical staff are more concerned with life saving at the time.

However this may be possible under controlled conditions. Robert Monroe, in his book *"Journeys out of the body"* gives detailed instructions how to project the spirit mind from the body, an ability he had developed and subsequently tutored others to do. (This is not analogous to lucid dreaming in which the dreamer is able to consciously influence the course of events in the dream.) While in the disembodied state, he could make detailed observations of the physical environment, which he confirmed subsequently. Just thinking of a person took him to them instantaneously, even though a large geographical distance separated them physically. He even managed to cause physical effects while in the projected state, which has profound implications (psychokinesis?). He was able to enter the realm of the afterlife and also another physical universe which superficially resembled our own but lacking any electrical technology. He found that his spirit mind responded slightly to earth's gravity (consistent with the apparent loss of body weight at death mentioned previously) but was strongly attracted to high tension power lines. This suggests that there is a significant electrical component to the spirit body. Others who have developed the ability to "astral project" in this manner report that when their physical body was placed in a Faraday cage at a high potential relative to the environment, their spirit body could not cross the electric field.

It seems the mind can be projected from the body during serious illness and also accidental traumas. There are many instances in which people involved in road accidents subsequently describe how they viewed the accident from above in a calm and almost unconcerned manner. They can describe accurately the activities of the rescue services dealing with the accident.

The spirit mind can be projected under the influence of drugs. The experiments with LSD show that subjects are projected, having a "trip", but the action of the drug can be harmful to the brain, so as a method of projecting the spirit mind it is not recommended. There are natural thresholds in each neuron of the brain that must be exceeded for signals to be transmitted. The action of LSD and other drugs is to lower these thresholds in a unselected manner so that stimuli (sensory and extrasensory) can flood the brain. The practice of meditation seems to permit these thresholds to be lowered selectively and consequently this is a safer procedure.

There are many methods of meditation. The transcendental method of meditation involves continuous repetition of a mantra or verbal sound and those who practice it report great feeling of relaxation and wellbeing, with an improved ability to cope with everyday living. Indeed, it seems that meditation generally improves both physical and mental health, and brings new insights into finding solutions to everyday problems.

These examples suggest that perhaps the mind can indeed exist independently of the body and therefore could survive beyond physical death. The Spiritualist movement has existed for the purpose of giving evidence supporting this principle. In this respect it differs from conventional religions in that it endeavours to provide evidence for this principle rather than rely on articles of faith. There is a huge bibliography citing evidence of survival, ranging from descriptions of the "dear departed", details of their lives and terminal illnesses, descriptions of articles passed down and perhaps misplaced, predictions of future opportunities for the embodied family member and advice concerning present personal problems. The activities of clairvoyants and clairaudients (who see and hear spirit respectively) are well known and documented. The members of other religions tend to be very critical of these psychics for various theological reasons, but one suspects there may be an element of jealousy that they are not so gifted and they feel that their religion is threatened in some way by these activities. An objective study of their religious literature shows that much of the prophetic material contained therein was due to the gifts of people whom we would today call "psychics", "clairvoyants" and "seers". Thus it seems that the mind is able to stand outside both three dimensional space and time.

Various occult (meaning hidden or concealed) sources present a model of human existence in which the spirit body is linked to the physical body by a "silver" cord, through which the physical body is controlled from the spirit body but which is broken at death. This cord is infinitely elastic, so that when the physical body is asleep, the spirit body is displaced to allow the spirit mind to rest and is able to travel at its own volition. Any disturbance of the physical body causes the "silver" cord to contract and return the spirit body to coincide with the physical. The "silver" cord links into the physical body in the brain, most probably at the brain stem or hypothalamus, and it is considered to be the route by which long-term memories are stored. (Robert Monroe observed his "silver" cord to be linked at the solar plexus, which may be the result of voluntarily induced projection.) At death, when the cord is broken (coinciding with the cessation of electrical activity in the brain stem), the spirit body carries with it the mind and life memories of the individual. Thus any deceased person may be able to communicate through the agency of a medium, which is the model proposed by Spiritualism.

It is appropriate at this point to provide a brief summary of the significance of the Spiritualist movement since it is very relevant to the question of the existence of the human mind without the body. During the nineteenth and early twentieth century, materialisation mediumship was quite commonplace within the movement. This is a term used to describe the ability of certain mediums to use their bodies to temporarily recreate the bodies of deceased people, as evidence of the afterlife to their relatives and loved ones. These mediums, when in deep trance, had the ability to extrude "ectoplasm" from bodily orifices from which the physical form of the deceased person was moulded. These materialisations were very variable in quality and quantity, some being full life-size, others miniature and only part body, just sufficient for the purpose of recognition. It seemed a necessary requirement for much of this activity to occur in total darkness or very dim illumination, which led many sceptics to suggest that it was fraudulent and that sitters were being duped. There were many instances of mediums being exposed as fraudulent, employing puppets and props or masquerading in costumes to mimic materialisations. Nevertheless, there were materialisation mediums who were proved to be genuine in their activities, often submitting to rigorous examination by eminent scientists such as Sir William Crookes, Sir Oliver Lodge and Sir William Barrett and author Sir Arthur Conan Doyle. It was the observations of these scientists that give a useful insight into these phenomena.

It seems that darkness or very subdued lighting was necessary for materialisation to occur (rather as light will fog a photographic film) since in seances where flash photography was employed, a rapid succession of flashes and exposures showed the materialisation receding rapidly and ectoplasm to be withdrawn back into the body of the medium. When the medium was secured to a chair which was placed on weighing scales, it was observed that up to a third of the medium's body weight was lost and the materialisation weighed the difference, so that mass appeared to be conserved throughout. The degree of materialisation might be as little as the superimposition of the deceased person's face upon that of the medium, a phenomenon known as transfiguration. I have witnessed transfiguration and recognised the face of my late father and also that of another person, from a photograph taken when he was alive. Their features bore no resemblance to those of the medium and remained fully formed for around five seconds. In this instance a bright red light was directed onto the medium's face so that there could be no possible trickery. It is conceivable that information for the likeness of the transfiguration is gleaned from the minds of the sitters, or that they are being hypnotised. I do not consider that I was hypnotised on that occasion, but was endeavouring to observe carefully. Those who witnessed whole body materialisations have touched them and reported that they feel warm and solid, with a pulse, just like a normal human body. Others who have tried to seize the materialisation or ectoplasm without permission caused it to be rapidly withdrawn into the medium's body and posed a serious risk to the medium's health (possible cardiac arrest). Indeed, the whole process was so demanding of the medium's strength that seances were necessarily infrequent, often no more than once per fortnight. Some mediums indulged in fraudulent imitations because they could not satisfy the public demand, particularly during periods of trauma and insecurity such as wartime.

An eminent classical scholar, Sir Frederick Myers, was the source of the "cross correspondences" after his death in 1931. He had been a single-minded investigator of evidence for survival of death during his later career, so it was in character that these communications occurred after his passing. A medium in Australia, a second medium in the USA and a third medium in the UK each received many fragmentary communications, which were written down, and each identified by the signature "Myers". The British medium had an understanding of Latin, so many communications through her were in this language. Subsequently, the three mediums made contact with each other by letter and only when the fragmentary communications were brought together did they make sense, with complete sentences, fitting like a jigsaw. The whole text extended to thousands of pages, written not just in English and Latin, but Greek and several other languages, so it was a huge undertaking to compile the fragments into a comprehensible whole. The complexity of this task, undertaken by the Society for Psychical Research, has caused this to be overlooked as perhaps the most convincing single piece of evidence for survival of death, raising the concept from the level of belief to one of knowledge.

Sir William Barrett compiled a dossier on deathbed visions, in which the person about to die, was able to communicate to those at the bedside visions of friends and relatives that had passed previously. In many instances, the passing of many of those identified in the visions was unknown to the person about to die, nor to the other family members at the bedside. Thus telepathy between living persons was eliminated as a source of these visions.

Another physical phenomenon that I have witnessed is "direct voice" mediumship. This involves the materialisation of just the voice box of the deceased person so that sound may be created and a conversation can occur first-hand between the deceased and the incarnate relative or friend. Some people consider this to be the most evidential form of mediumship. The resulting conversations seemed to be very natural, but the sound level of the voice from the materialised larynx varied from a whisper to a shout, as though the deceased person was deaf but responding to the thoughts (telepathy) of the sitter. The room was pitch dark but crowded with around seventy sitters, so that it would have been impossible for the medium to have moved around without tripping over people's legs. A sceptical explanation of this phenomenon could be ventriloquism, but it struck me that it was unlikely that a ventriloquist could project his voice so far across a crowded room, discussing intimate matters with various sitters, and mimicking the voice and accent of the deceased so realistically.

The hazards to the health of the mediums posed by the various forms of physical mediumship have caused these phenomena to become rare. Also the opinion has grown within the Spiritualist movement that mental mediumship offers better evidence of survival of death. The materialisation phenomena demanded a degree of commitment on the part of the medium and sitters that is not common today, where Western lifestyles present too many distractions. For example, one materialisation group in Canada during the 1930s held twice-weekly sittings for a decade with no absences by any members. This group were successful in producing photographs of mostly miniature materialisations, taken with both flash and infrared cameras.

An objective observer of Spiritualist phenomena may not be convinced that what is presented as evidence of survival is just that; there are alternative theories. Scientific models are chosen to be the most simple consistent with the phenomenon being observed. Presently, the model presented by Spiritualists is the simplest (i.e., that "dead" people can communicate) and alternative explanations for all the various phenomena tend to become very complicated.

Mind outside time

"Mother" Shipton's Prophecy,
Knaresborough, Yorkshire, UK, 1488-1561.

And now a word in couth rhyme
Of what shall be in future time
For, in those wonderous far off days
The women shall adopt a craze
To dress like men and trousers wear
And cut off all their locks of hair
They'll ride astride with brazen brow
As witches do, on broomsticks now.
Then love shall die and marriage cease
And nations wane as babes decrease.
Then wives will fondle cats and dogs
And men shall live the same as hogs.
A carriage without horse shall go.
Accidents fill the world with woe.
In London Primrose Hill shall be
Its centre hold a bishop's see.
Around the world men's thoughts shall fly
Quick as the twinkling of an eye
And waters shall great wonders do
How strange and that it shall come true
The upside down the world shall be
And gold found at the root of tree
Through towering hills proud men shall ride,
No horse or mule by his side
Beneath the water men shall walk
Shall ride, shall sleep and even talk

And in the air men shall be seen
In white, in black as well as green
A great man shall come and go
For prophecy declares it so
In water iron shall then float
As easy as a wooden boat.
Gold shall be found in streams and stone
In land that is as yet unknown
Water and fire shall wonders do
And England shall admit a Jew   *(1948 Palestine Mandate)*
The Jew that once was held in scorn
Shall of a Christian then be born   *(Most Israelis are Europeans)*
A house of glass shall come to pass   *(Crystal Palace, 1906)*
In England — but alas! alas!
A war will follow with the work
Where dwells the pagan and the Turk   *(1914-18 World War 1)*
The states will lock in fiercest strife
And seek to take each other's life
When the north shall thus divide the south   *(Colonial exploitation)*
The eagle build in lion's mouth   *(USA replaces UK as major world power)*
The tax and blood in cruel war
Shall come to every humble door   *(1939-45 World War 2, bombing of cities)*
Then when the fiercest fight is done
England and France shall be as one   *(European Community)*
The British olive next shall twine
In marriage with the German line   *(British Royal Family)*
Men shall walk beneath and over streams
Fulfilled will be our strangest dreams
All England's sons that plough the land
Shall oft be seen with book in hand   *(Universal education)*
The poor shall now great wisdom know
Great houses stand in far flung vale
All covered o'er with snow and hail
In nineteen hundred and twenty-six
Build houses light with straw and sticks   *(Thatched houses)*
For then shall mighty wars be planned   *(Cold War, West v Soviet Union)*
When pictures seem alive with movements free
When boats like fishes swim beneath the sea
When men like birds shall scour the sky
Then half this world deep drenched in blood shall be

But those who live to see this through
In fear and trembling this will do
Flee to the mountains and the dens
To bog and forest and wild fens
For storms will rage and oceans roar   *(Climate change)*
When Gabriel stands on sea and shore
And as he blows his wondrous horn
Old worlds shall die and new be born.

The sense of time is defined by the sequence of events and our lives are ruled by the system based on the rotation of the earth on its axis and its revolution about the sun. It was Einstein in his theory of relativity that showed that time was variable, dependent on the speed of the observer. Since we are located on the surface of a sphere, rotating at 1,600 km/hour at the equator and at over 100,000 km/hour in its orbit around the sun, we are most certainly not stationary. Our solar system is located on the edge of the Milky Way galaxy, which is itself rotating at even greater speed. Hence our system of time in relation to stars observed across our galaxy or in other galaxies will be quite different. The past, present and future in distant places will most certainly not coincide with ours. Since light from these distant stars reaches us at a constant speed of 300 million m/second, what we observe now is the position of these stars in the past, at a time when the light we receive in our present was emitted by them. In effect, the further we look out into the universe, the further back in time we travel, and the distant universe at this moment will be quite different from what we observe.

However, relativity concerns itself with the rate at which we proceed from the present into the future. It does not have anything to say about how we may shape that future by choices made in the present. Indeed, there seems to be a sense in which certain aspects of the future may be predefined and limits may be prescribed on our ability to make changes in the present. This suggests that there may be a master plan for the human race and the future of this planet. As individuals we have free will to make our futures in the present but collectively we may be constrained. Certain individuals throughout our history have been gifted with insights of the collective destiny, and have made prophecies. These individuals tend not to be popular with the contemporary elite, who feel threatened by their pronouncements.

One body of evidence lies in the ability to predict events. Where these concern the individual, they are the logical result of the course in life the person is taking. However, within the present, we each have free will, so that we are able to change our course and therefore change our future. In the affairs of whole nations, changes of direction are less common (the inertia posed by millions of competing and conflicting free wills), so that the prediction of world events is less prone to error. In this respect the recently deciphered "Bible Code" is interesting. The first five books of the Old Testament, the Pentateuch, written by the prophet Moses, was originally an unpunctuated text of over 300,000 Hebrew characters. This has been meticulously reproduced by Hebrew scholars over the centuries so that today we can have reasonable confidence that it is unchanged from Moses' original text. Sir Isaac Newton suspected that these ancient texts contained a hidden code and he spent many years trying to decipher it. He lacked a computer. With the aid of computers, it has been possible to arrange the text in such a manner that significant words and phrases relating to contemporary events are aligned vertically or diagonally across the lines of text. Thus the assassination of Israeli prime minister Yitzhak Rabin on 4th November 1995 was highlighted just before the actual event but too late to avert it. The texts are still being decoded but the portents for the Middle East are ominous. (A similar analysis of a Hebrew translation of *"War and Peace"* by Tolstoy showed no such significant correlations.) Some people think that later books of the Old Testament may be similarly encoded but it is unlikely that the New Testament is similarly encoded. The history of Christianity shows that much editing of texts was carried out for religio-political reasons. The one exception to this is the Book of Revelations, which probably escaped the censorship of the Council of Nicea (in AD 330 under the Emperor Constantine) because no one present could understand it. Its apocalyptic language gained it a certain respect!

At the beginning of this section, the fifteenth century prophecy of Ursula Shipton of Knaresborough, Yorkshire, UK was quoted. It describes quite clearly events of the twentieth century as seen from an English perspective, and precedes the encoded prophecies of Nostradamus. For her clarity of vision and expression and independence of mind she was burned at the stake as a witch and heretic. Nostradamus avoided such a fate by making his prophecies so obscure that no one in authority could understand them.

Throughout history there have been countless people blessed with timeless vision, who most often fell foul of those in authority. St Malachy was stricken with a strange illness in the year 1173 that caused him to utter prophecies, which were written down. These were concealed from the public by the Catholic Church authorities for 450 years for understandable reasons and only recently were published. Among the many predictions relating to our present, there are to be only two more Popes after John Paul 2nd, whereupon the Church will be disestablished. Already people are deserting the established Churches in significant numbers. Nostradamus predicted an invasion of Europe from Asia in the twenty-first century. The flow of economic refugees and asylum seekers from that part of the world into Europe has already started. This will be a source of considerable ethnic and religious trouble.

There is a statistically significant number of passengers that fail to take ill-fated flights, bus and train journeys. It seems that these people have premonitions that an accident will occur. The motto "to be forewarned is to be forearmed" is very true.

Our understanding of the natural world allows predictions to be made based on scientific principles. However the knowledge of geophysics is not yet sufficient to allow predictions of the occurrence of earthquakes and volcanic eruptions, for which populations can be moved out of danger. It may be possible for psychics to pinpoint likely periods of maximum risk, but for the most part, where timing is concerned, they tend not to be very accurate. This is probably because no system of time as we know it exists in the domain from this information is gleaned. This then leaves the possibility of relocating populations permanently away from danger zones.

In the case of the collapse of the volcano on La Palma in the Canary Isles, and the resultant mega tsunami that could destroy the eastern US coastal cities and flood low lying areas of Europe, the zones and populations at risk are so great that a forewarning of hours would be impracticable. The transportation systems of all countries at risk would become gridlocked. The relocation and resettlement of the populations concerned, including New York, Washington DC, London and Paris would be horrendously expensive unless carried out over several years, for which the various national defence budgets would be required. The volcano erupted in 1949 and in 1971, so that the next eruption is overdue. Perhaps the most cost effective measure would be to engage on massive earthworks to remove the unstable western flank of the volcano so that the next eruption cannot cause a significant tsunami. This would have to be an international undertaking.

The images of the future received by many are of massive flooding of the major coastal and low lying cities of Europe and the USA. In the case of New York, the towers of Manhattan were wrecked. The disaster movies may be a presentation of these premonitions. London and Paris became like Venice, with a limited amount of traffic in boats and a huge loss of life. But these images are not inevitable if steps are taken to avert the cause. The governments are rightly concerned not to create mass panic, but it is equally imprudent to ignore such warnings.

Thus we have ample evidence that the human mind, from Moses to the present day, can exist beyond time. There is a human need for reassurance about the future, and this faculty has been latent within us to fulfil that need. We have the free will to take steps that can avert those threatening possibilities.

Mind in Nature

It is assumed in contemporary society that *Homo sapiens* are the peak of the evolutionary process, in possessing intelligence and self-awareness. Yet a closer examination of flora and fauna most clearly shows the working of intelligence.

In Charles Darwin's *"Origin of Species"*, a process of natural selection is described whereby each species of plant and animal alive today has survived as the result of adaptation to its environment. These adaptations are the result of trial and error, in which erroneous adaptations result in extinction. Thus we see the successful adaptations only. This process is attributed to chance mutations, which over eons of time, the unsuccessful changes are weeded out. The success or otherwise of an adaptation depends on food supply, climate changes, predators and migration.

However, closer inspection of natural selection shows intelligence applied in the evolutionary process. Each species survives because of developed abilities that transcend those of humans in many ways. It is arrogance to assume that humans are the most intelligent, since intelligence may take many forms, not necessarily characterised by spoken and written language and analytical thought.

Birds migrate over thousands of miles navigating by the stars or the earth's magnetic field. For such migrations, the conservation of energy is vital. By flying in a "vee" formation the leading birds create an uplift for the birds behind, saving up to 70% of energy expenditure. The birds take turns in the lead so as to share the workload, ensuring that the maximum number will reach their destination.

Whales communicate with infrasound across thousands of miles of ocean, using warm layers of water to channel their signals. These communications indicate number, gender and food sources, thereby promoting survival.

Swarms of bees and wasps can locate sources of nectar at considerable distances. Colonies of termites respond instantly to any disturbance in their territories, suggestive of a system of collective telepathy. Chameleons and various species of octopus can change colour to effectively camouflage themselves against changing backgrounds, which implies a system of self-awareness.

In the armoury of self-defence, elaborate schemes have been devised. One species of frog has developed a binary chemical weapon, in which two harmless substances are mixed, to produce an irritant which is squirted at any potential predator. The most deadly toxins known have been produced in nature's continuing battle for attack and defence. Some of mankind's most effective technical designs have been modelled on nature.

The development of modern science and technology has been the result of trial and error, constructing theories, modifying them or developing new theories to account for observations. It would seem that a similar process operates in nature, in which an underlying intelligence or intelligences are at work. These intelligences may operate through invisible energy fields that can influence the structure of water, and thereby make small and subtle changes to DNA. It may be that a collective unconscious mind associated with each species is responsible for this process, but the time scale over which many of these changes occur may be too long for them to be readily observed in a laboratory.

It is well known that viruses and bacteria mutate in response to the environment, and there is always a minority that adapts to survive any drug or antibiotic treatment. Our defence has traditionally been that the resistant minority has had to compete with the non-resistant majority for limited nutritional resources. With the elimination of the non-resistant majority, the minority pose a significant threat to humanity and drug research becomes increasingly preoccupied with counter measures for these resistant strains. Since these mutations occur in water, it is possible that changes to the water itself may prevent the mutations from occurring.

Finale

I write these words in the aftermath of the destruction of the World Trade Centre in New York and damage to the Pentagon in Washington by terrorists on the 11th of September 2001. This event is very significant since it marks the beginning of the Third World War. Each world war has created a new world order and this war will do likewise. It will be a great leveller, in which the affluent West will no longer dominate the world economy. The world will become a more level playing field for all nations.

There is an epidemic afflicting the majority of mankind at the present. It is fear. Fear is the opposite of love, and creates enmity and distrust. This fear is afflicting financial markets and air travel at this time. There is now a fear of terrorism using weapons of mass destruction, chemical and biological and nuclear since there is an increasing concentration of populations in cities which are more vulnerable to such attack.

Fear manifests as xenophobia, distrust of other religious and ethnic groups and so provides the basis of conflict and warfare. This is possible because there is a failure of perception that has resulted from religious indoctrination, so that this planet is populated by spiritually blind and immature souls. Spiritual growth is a natural process that can be impeded by religious indoctrination, since the latter can confuse the individual with irrelevant information. Consider the large number of religiously-based centres of education in the world. They are designed to perpetuate the cultures and prejudices of the parents. Yet in truth, all that is required is the teaching of comparative religion and its historical significance, tolerance, a respect for all forms of life, the teaching of cause and effect and personal responsibility. Many will feel threatened by

74

this statement, yet for the future survival of the human race, this must occur. There is no place for religious fundamentalism, of any persuasion, since religion divides people from each other. Spirituality unites people. In this sense, religion and spirituality are opposites.

"Most people's minds are like concrete, thoroughly mixed and permanently set". Where religion is concerned, this is especially true. Religions teach questionable histories, with edited texts subject to considerable misinterpretations and misunderstandings. A wise spiritually aware person does not take such teachings too seriously.

There is a need in mankind to worship an all powerful deity, and evidence for the existence of this can be seen in the subtleties and wonders of the natural world. We are part of this natural world and can wonder at the intelligence manifest in nature and in the construction and function of our bodies. This is true for all people of all religions. All our needs are met on this planet, and deprivation of needs are the result of man's inhumanity and greed. This is a pivotal moment in the affairs of mankind; war will destroy life and property on an unprecedented scale reducing those who survive to a Stone-Age existence. However, if a spiritual approach is adopted by world leaders and their peoples, with a sharing of resources, everyone gains. We are all connected.

The electronic internet mirrors the existence of the universal unconscious mind, in which all knowledge resides and into which we can all tap. Regardless of ethnicity, religion, skin colour or language, the process of daily meditation brings peace, reassurance (abolishing fear), upliftment and renewal. We are never alone. Each has a spiritual umbilicus to the universal Mind. Sadly, for the majority, this is unknown territory. Hence there is a need to write this book, in the hope that readers will start to explore the inner universe. The only dictum is "Man, know thyself". If the construction and function of the physical body is a source of wonder, just consider the even greater wonders of the energy body that maintains it and the spirit body that is the repository of our life memories and experiences. The spiritual awareness gleaned by this inner exploration guides all decision making in this increasingly complex world that we have created. Without this guidance we are doomed to self-destruction. The course of events now unfolding will leave mankind with no choice but to become spiritually aware or face extinction. We seem to be at war with each other and with the planet itself. We have discovered that the earth goes through natural cycles involving rapid changes of climate. We interfere with these at our peril.

This need not be a time of fear but one of great hope since the changes being forced upon humanity leave no choice but to become spiritually aware, to share resources among all people. The process of globalisation cannot be resisted if it is concerned with sharing and not domination. Respect of different cultures is not in conflict with a spiritually-based globalisation. We have been given the opportunity at this time not to repeat the mistakes of the past. With spiritual awareness we stand to create a golden age, in which knowledge is tempered by spiritual wisdom. Our inner exploration has only just begun!

MY LAW: Tieme Ranapiri

The sun may be clouded, yet ever the sun
Will sweep on its course till the cycle is run.
And when into chaos the system is hurled,
Again shall the Builder re-shape a new world.

Your path may be clouded, uncertain your goal,
Move on — for your orbit is fixed to your soul.
And though it may lead to the darkness of night,
The torch of the Builder shall give it new light.

You were, you will be, know this while you are.
Your spirit has travelled both long and afar,
It came from the source, to the source it returns
The spark which was lighted eternally burns.

It slept in the jewel, it leapt in a wave,
It roamed in the forest, it rose from the grave.
It took on strange garbs for long eons of years,
And now in the soul of yourself it appears.

From body to body your spirit moves on,
It seeks a new form when the old one has gone,
And the form that it finds is the fabric you wrought
On the loom of the mind from the fabric of thought.

As the dew is drawn upwards, in rain to descend,
Your thoughts drift away and in destiny blend.
You can never escape them, for petty or great,
Or evil or noble, they fashion your fate.

Somewhere on some planet, sometime and somehow,
Your life will reflect your thoughts of the now.
My law is unerring, no blood can atone,
The structure you built you will live in alone.

From cycle to cycle, through time and through space,
Your lives with your longings will ever keep pace,
And all that you ask for, and all you desire
Must come at your bidding, as flames out of fire.

Once list to that voice and all tumult is done,
Your life is the life of the infinite one,
In the hurrying pace you are conscious of pause,
With love for the purpose and love for the cause.

You are your own devil, you are your own God,
You fashioned the paths your footsteps have trod.
And no one can save you from error or sin
Until you have harkened to the spirit within.

(Attributed to a Maori)

Further Reading

"Nature's network, interdependence in nature", Keith Reid, Aldus Books, 1969.

"Journeys out of the body", Robert A. Monroe, Doubleday and Co. Inc., New York, 1972; Souvenir Press, London, 1972, 1986.

"Supernature", Lyall Watson, Coronet Books/ Hodder paperbacks Ltd., 1974.

"The Romeo Error", Lyall Watson, Hodder and Stoughton Ltd., 1974; Coronet Edition 1976.

"Vision tomorrow", Edmund Harold, Greenhouse Publications Pty Ltd., Richmond, Victoria, Australia, 1981, 1986, 1988.

"Supernature 2", Lyall Watson, Sceptre Books, 1987.

"A brief history of time", Stephen Hawking, Bantam Press, 1988.

"The Holographic Universe", Michael Talbot, Harper Collins, 1991; Harper Perennial, 1992.

"Antarctica, Warnings from the ice", Time, March 1997, p86-91.

"The Bible Code", Michael Drosnin, Weidenfeld and Nicholson, 1997.

"The world to come", Lloyd Geering, Bridget Williams Books Ltd., Wellington, New Zealand, 1998.

"Untangling the science of climate change", Curt Suplee, *National Geographic*, May 1998, p44-71.

"Chill in the air", New Scientist, 1st May 1999, p29-32.

"The greatest apes", Karen Hopkin, *New Scientist*, 15th May 1999, p28-30.

"Is global warming harmful to health?", Paul R. Epstein, *Scientific American*, August 2000, p36-43.

"The drowning wave", Tristan Marshall, *New Scientist*, 7th October 2000, p26-30.

"Smart Proteins", Phil Jones, *New Scientist* Supplement, 17th March 2001.

New Scientist Global Environment Supplement, April 2001.

"Life force", Mark Buchanan, *New Scientist*, 15th April 2001, p21-24.

"Hype, hope and healing", *New Scientist*, 20th May 2001, p29-53.

"No limits", Alison Motluk, *New Scientist*, 11th August 2001, p24-28.

"You must remember this", Bryant Furlow, *New Scientist*, 13th September 2001, p25-27.

"The hollow universe", J. R. Minkel, *New Scientist*, 27th April 2002, p 22-26.